INTIMACY
WITH
GOD

A Journey into a Life
of Supernatural Experience

FEMI AGBOOLA

Trilogy Christian Publishers

A Wholly Owned Subsidiary of Trinity Broadcasting Network

2442 Michelle Drive

Tustin, CA 92780

For information, address Trilogy Christian Publishing

Rights Department, 2442 Michelle Drive, Tustin, Ca 92780.

Trilogy Christian Publishing/ TBN and colophon are trademarks of Trinity Broadcasting Network.

For information about special discounts for bulk purchases, please contact Trilogy Christian Publishing.

Trilogy Disclaimer: The views and content expressed in this book are those of the author and may not necessarily reflect the views and doctrine of Trilogy Christian Publishing or the Trinity Broadcasting Network.

10 9 8 7 6 5 4 3 2 1

Library of Congress Cataloging-in-Publication Data is available.

ISBN 979-8-89041-768-8

ISBN 979-8-89041-769-5 (ebook)

DEDICATION

To my wife, Yemi, and our precious children: Ayo, Tope, Femi, and Dara.

This book is dedicated to each and every one of you who has been the source of love, support, and inspiration throughout our journey together.

Yemi, your love and constant belief in me have been the driving force behind every page written, every dream pursued, and every milestone achieved. You are not only my cheerleader but also my partner and closest friend.

Ayo, Tope, Femi, and Dara, watching you grow, witnessing your unique personalities blossom, and being a part of your lives have been the greatest blessings I could ever receive as a father. Your curiosity, resilience, and kindness constantly inspire me to be a better person.

This dedication serves as a token of my gratitude and a testament to the unbreakable bond we share. Thank you for standing by my side with unwavering encouragement and loving me without conditions. Without you, this book would not have been possible.

With all my love,
Femi.

ACKNOWLEDGEMENT

I would like to express my heartfelt gratitude to the following individuals who have played significant roles in my journey and in making this book a reality:

My mom, Mrs. Elizabeth Agboola, for your love and support for me and my siblings after my dad passed. Thank you for staying strong for the family. Pastor Ebenezer and Deaconess Rachel Adu, I call you Mommy and Daddy. Thank you for your unwavering support, encouragement, and love throughout this journey.

My spiritual parents, Pastor (Dr.) Patrick and Prophetess Mabel Odigie, whose guidance and mentorship have been invaluable in shaping my spiritual growth and understanding.

Pastor (Prof.) Samuel O. & Deaconess Janet K. Ajayi. The Gospel Faith Mission International (GOFAMINT), Ado Ekiti, Nigeria, for your guidance in the early stages of my journey. The godly counsel, prayers, and continuous belief in me meant a lot to me. People like you are very rare in our world today. I will forever remember your labor of love.

Pastor E.O Oluwanimotele (Regional Pastor). The Gospel Faith Mission International (GOFAMINT), Akure, Ondo State, Nigeria. You have always been a great source of encouragement in my journey. Thank you for your continuous belief in me and the call of God upon my life.

Thank you all for your unwavering support and encouragement. You have been a constant source of inspiration for me. I am forever grateful for your presence in my life. Thank you all for being a part of this remarkable journey!

To my dearest wife, our journey together started more than three decades ago. It feels like just yesterday when we were teenagers in the church (GOFAMINT, Ado Ekiti) we both attended. Little did we know then that we would be partners in this beautiful journey of faith and devotion. Even back then, when we borrowed Christian books from the library and from friends, I would make sure that both of us read the book. Sometimes, you would hand copy an entire book so that we could have a copy of it for a later review because the owner wanted the books back sooner than I could finish reading it. I still have copies of those hand-written books. They are a reminder of God's faithfulness. I cannot express how grateful I am for the countless hours you spent proofreading and editing the drafts of *Intimacy with God*. I am forever grateful to God for your presence in my life.

ENDORSEMENTS
A FIRSTHAND WITNESS

I've waited three decades for this book! Since I met you as a young man, you have had a zeal for God that was "strange" to your contemporaries. You have been my mentor and best friend for decades, and I am privileged to be a firsthand witness to many of the experiences you shared in this book.

Introducing me to the pursuit of intimacy with God is one of the lifetime blessings I've received from being around you. I see how developing intimacy with God has shaped your life and priorities over the years. Your lifestyle of intentionally hosting God's presence encourages me to seek the Holy Spirit daily.

Thank you for mirroring the Father's love for me and our children.

It is heartwarming to see you sharing your journey and experiences with your readers. Sharing these truths will help each reader to experience what I've witnessed firsthand. At times, we are unaware of the possibilities that await us in Christ. At other times, we know the possibilities, but they seem so unreachable. In this book, you seamlessly bridged both gaps. Readers will not only see the immense depth of the love of the Father through this work but also how to connect with His love on an intimate level. "Intimacy with God" is more than a book; it is an experience. It is indeed a joy to read! Thank you for writing this book!

—Yemi Agboola

The book "Intimacy with God" serves as a cherished gift bestowed upon God's children during a time when we have collectively distanced ourselves from Him, engrossed in the pursuit of worldly matters. Pastor Femi deserves gratitude for allowing himself to be a vessel in the hands of God for such a significant task. As I delved into the pages of this book, a sense of nostalgia washed over me, echoing the call of a loving Father to His wayward children. I encountered this book precisely when I yearned for intimacy and reassurance from God.

Through the pages, I came to realize that our intimacy with the Father hinges on accepting His profound love for us and acknowledging the role of that love in drawing us nearer to Him. The Holy Spirit, through Pastor Femi, guided us back to the realm of agape love and resounding fellowship with the Father. "Intimacy with God" serves as a poignant reminder of His original plan for humanity before the fall. Pastor Femi, with the assistance of the Holy Spirit, adeptly connects our hunger for God with the profound impact of His love. The book elucidates the reality of His love and its pivotal role in fostering intimacy with Him, establishing His love as the bedrock for our identity in Christ.

I highly recommend this book to every believer who yearns for intimacy with God.

—Pastor Adebayo Adebambo
RCCG House Of Praise
Chesapeake, Virginia

This book is an essential read for anyone who longs for deeper intimacy with God, no matter where you are in your relationship with Jesus. As you read, you will not only be challenged to build your faith in Christ Jesus, but it will also challenge you to make intimacy with God a lifestyle that will move you with excitement to share the love of God with the people you meet. There is truly no other love greater than the love of God.

The author is so transparent as he shares his experiences and his desire for God; he also takes us on a journey on this experience with him on how God filled his void after a great loss. God can fill every void in our lives, and He wants to draw us closer to Himself so we can experience His love. I am greatly blessed and inspired after reading this book. I couldn't put it down, and I am encouraged to live a lifestyle of intimacy with God. This book is intriguing, and it is what we all need right now in the body of Christ. It is certainly a must-read.

—Krisie Stanley
Canada

Is there a hunger in you to shift from being an ordinary Christian to experiencing the supernatural every day? Do you desire to enjoy a closer walk with God the Father, God the Son, and God the Holy Spirit? Are you desiring to become addicted to prayer? Do you want to take worship to a greater height? Is your heart desire to exchange your will with God's will for your life? If your answer to each of the questions is "yes," then I strongly encourage you to read this book, "Intimacy with God."

The uniqueness of this book is that it was birthed through the author's personal encounter with the Holy Spirit in the place of worship. The author shared a practical experience of "draw near to God, and He will draw near to you" (James 4:8a) that happened during *his early walk with God. This initial occurrence later became an everyday episode that revolutionized the author's personal prayer life.*

—Dr. Gloria Ezeala
High School Teacher/Financial Professional
Richmond, Virginia

Since the beginning of time, it has been the intention of Creator God, our loving Father, to be in deep, intimate, unbroken fellowship and relationship with us, His creation, His beloved children.

This book takes us on a journey into the heart of the Father. It unpacks the living Word of God to give us a greater understanding of the Father's will and purpose for our lives. It explores His perfect plan from creation to the cross. Then, it unravels the things in our personal lives that may be hindering us from growing deeper in close relationship with Him.

Through his personal testimony of experiencing and encountering God, through his years of wisdom and revelation as a student of the Word and exploration into the heart of God, through this book, Femi reveals love in its purest form, Jesus, the worthy Lamb of God. Including all that life offers when we truly live a life surrendered unto Him.

This book is an invitation for you, no matter where you are on your faith journey, to receive this gift of salvation, the gift of deliverance and freedom, and encourages you to walk daily in the transforming power of the spirit.

When we know who we are, that we are loved and destined for a glorious hope, then we can extend that love to others, we can say "yes" and partner with heaven to see His purposes, His plan, and, most importantly, His heart manifested in our lives, in our families, and all throughout the world.

—Aimee Ruth Bell
Hearts of Fire Ministries
Australia

The journey of life demands intentionality. Your existence on Earth is not by chance; you did not appear on Earth by accident. You are unique to God. As I write this, the world currently holds over 8 billion, and none of us have the same fingerprint. Thus, you are unique to God. You are "fearfully and wonderfully made" (Psalm 139:14). You are filled with wonder and beauty of your Heavenly Father—God. This beauty shines brighter and better when you dwell in the secret place of the Most High.

This book shows us how God's love towards us is immeasurable and that God's love does not discriminate regardless of who you are. God made you in His image and cannot trade you for other things. He values you just like He values His Son, Jesus Christ. No matter who you are or how big you think your sin is, Jesus is always waiting for you; His love is indispensable. You need to read this book to discover that Jesus has not given up on you, and His arms are always open to welcome you to the Kingdom of His Father.

"Intimacy with God" is a book that takes you back to the greatest book in history (the Bible). Nothing brings unspeakable joy to a man or woman than to read the Bible for themselves. I encourage you to have this book next to your Bible, and if you are not a Christian, please read this book with an open heart and give God a chance because your life journey requires intimacy with God—Your Creator. This must be done intentionally.

After salvation, there is a need for sanctification; this book allows you to invite Jesus into your life and encourages you to trust Jesus with your life. This book is a must-have for believers interested in being set apart for God. It is a book that enables you to continue working towards perfection.

As Pastor Femi said, "The invitation to respond to God's love is not passive. It calls for action, for a conscious decision to open our hearts and minds to the transformative power of this love." I encourage you to read this book and get a copy for yourself, friends, families, and co-workers. This book is an evangelism tool. No one has gone beyond a state of redemption. Jesus Christ awaits you even as you read and meditate through the pages of this book.

—Solomon Oluwabiyi
Viewpoint Ministries International
Maryland, USA

The author has made my understanding of relationship with God more alive and more complete. God is real, and He loves me and wants a deep personal relationship with me. Not just once in a while, but daily, all the time! After reading this, I want to know even more about God's desires and love for my life and my relationship with Him to grow much deeper.

This has also made me revisit my salvation and the great price that has been paid for my life, my eternal salvation. I'm again humbled and overwhelmed by God's love for me, for us.

—Pattie Brockley
Rob 3/10 Ministry
Norfolk, Virginia, USA

Femi Agboola is among the most passionate individuals I've encountered during our time in leadership school. His profound devotion to worship and to God permeates his life, evident in the essence of this writing. The book is enriched with profound scriptural teachings, delivering a much-needed message on the Father's love. The eternal themes of God's love, intimacy, and the Father's embrace are beautifully portrayed through Femi's perspective, for which I am truly grateful. I trust that this book will inspire and encourage you. I highly recommend it!

—Sang Pulidindi
Bethel School of Supernatural Ministry
Reading, California, USA

God's purpose from creation is to have companionship with man. This was demonstrated in the Garden of Eden when He would sometimes visit the first man, Adam, in the garden and have fellowship with him. God had always yearned for that close relationship with man. He wanted man to live in a sincere love relationship with Him, but unfortunately, man failed in this responsibility!

However, this opportunity lost was brought back to man through the saving grace of our Lord Jesus Christ! Hallelujah! Unfortunately, many believers in Christ are actually missing this aspect of their true identity in Christ. By the grace of God, this book titled "Intimacy with God" is an eye opener to the "no struggle" or "stressless" way of having an intimate relationship with God as personally experienced by the man of God, the writer of this book.

Pastor Femi has been known through the years to have a consistent walk with the Lord, hence the grace to share his personal encounter regarding the meaning, purpose, importance, and the blessings attached to having an intimate relationship with God, which is brought out of genuine love for God that surpasses our understanding transforming us from the inside out, hallelujah!

Dear reader, I congratulate you as you are about to read this book, which reveals that having an intimate relationship with God means realizing that your abundant life will never be found in another person but Christ. God bless you!

—Dr. Olubunmi Ojo
New Jersey, USA

TABLE OF CONTENTS

PREFACE
A LIFE OF SUPERNATURAL EXPERIENCE

You are welcome! This volume, *Intimacy with God*, is a book that invites you on a journey toward building a genuine connection with our Heavenly Father. Although greatly condensed, it is a record of years of personal encounters with the love of the Father, coupled with references from the holy Scriptures. Amid the hustle and bustle of life, we often lose sight of the awe-inspiring and life-changing bond that is within our reach with our Creator. This captivating book addresses the longing within each of us for a relationship that goes beyond human comprehension.

The title *Intimacy with God* signifies not only a yearning but also an intense desire to truly know and understand our Heavenly Father—a God who is neither distant nor abstract but rather lovingly personal. As we embark on this journey, we will uncover a longing within ourselves—for something greater—that calls us to achieve a deeper understanding of God's unwavering presence in every aspect of our daily lives.

Throughout the pages of this book, we will delve into the timeless truths found in the holy Scriptures. It is through these words that we receive guidance, solace, and revelations. They speak directly to the depths of our hearts, resonating with the yearning for intimacy with our Father.

In *Intimacy with God*, we will come across stories, reflections, and practical insights that will lead us on this path of closeness. We will learn how to nurture a prayer life, embrace the power of worship and spiritual growth, understand the significance of the Holy Spirit's presence, and learn how to walk in the anointing that God has so generously granted to His children. Additionally, we will explore how to overcome obstacles that may hinder our connection with God.

I warmly welcome you to open your heart and mind as we embark on this journey together. Let's delve into the power of intimacy and experience the joy that accompanies a relationship with our Heavenly Father.

May this book be a guide and source of inspiration as you navigate toward an intimate bond with God. As we plunge into the depths of *Intimacy with God*, may we uncover the blessings that await us along this path.

INTRODUCTION

A CALL TO A DEEPER RELATIONSHIP WITH THE HEAVENLY FATHER

It was during one of our evening prayer meetings back in 1992. I was to lead praise and worship before our Wednesday prayer meeting. As usual, I got up and walked gently to the front of the hall full of students. There were no musical instruments, no microphones, or media, but the hall was filled with the sound of our voices and thunderous hand claps, with a deep longing in our hearts for God.

I did not know what was about to happen. I had led worship countless times before this meeting, so I wasn't expecting anything spectacular to happen. Unknown to me, what I was about to experience would forever alter my life as a believer. As I began singing, I noticed that my voice and the words of the songs were inadequate to convey the depth of what I was feeling on the inside. A feeling that no human vocabulary can describe. Suddenly, I felt a warm liquid rolling down my cheek. It was an indescribable joy. At the same time, I wasn't sure how to respond to the new experience. It was all strange to me, but I didn't want it to stop. With my eyes closed, I continued worshipping. I noticed that the people started to sing louder. When I opened my eyes, I saw people singing uncontrollably, some on their knees and worshiping. What a glorious sight! After the meeting, I quickly returned to my small room, puzzled by the experience. I said to myself that whatever that was, I wanted more!

I opened my mouth to pray and noticed it wasn't a struggle. I stayed up most of that night praying. I wanted that moment to linger forever, but I had to attend classes the following day. The thought of this new experience filled my mind all day. I could not wait to get back to my room for another taste of this new experience. It became my longing each day. My personal devotion took another dimension. An unexplainable hunger for a deeper knowledge of God was generated within me. I could stay longer in the place of prayer and communion with God. This became my daily routine for several months.

My eyes became opened to several possibilities in God that I never knew existed or thought it was reserved for a selected few. I realized that I was created for intimacy with my King. I later came to understand that the Father had been waiting all this while for me to embrace His love and the invitation for a closer walk with Him. He initiates every experience of intimacy we have with Him. He started pursuing us before the creation of the world.

> Blessed be the God and Father of our Lord Jesus Christ, who has blessed us with every spiritual blessing in the heavenly places in Christ, just as He chose us in Him before the foundation of the world, that we should be holy and without blame before Him in love, having predestined us to adoption as sons by Jesus Christ to Himself, according to the good pleasure of His will,
>
> Ephesians 1:3–5 (NKJV)

Our hunger for intimacy isn't something we came up with; rather, it is our response to the invitation that has been there all along.

"Blessed is the man You choose, And cause to approach You, That he may dwell in Your courts. We shall be satisfied with the goodness of Your house, Of Your holy temple" (Psalm 65:4, NKJV).

We are called to a deeper relationship with God. God is not abstract. He is the creator who longs to be with His children. In the depths of our souls, there lies a longing for something greater, something more profound than the mundane routines of life. It is a yearning for a connection that transcends human understanding, a desire to be intimately acquainted with our Creator. This desire, this call, beckons us to embark on a journey toward a deeper relationship with the Heavenly Father, the source of all life and love. His holy Words, the Scripture, speak to the depths of our hearts, resonating with the timeless truth that guides our souls.

The Psalmist writes, "As the deer pants for the water brooks, So pants my soul for You, O God" (Psalm 42:1, NKJV).

These words echo the longing that resides within each of us, the thirst for a union with our Creator that brings satisfaction and fulfillment beyond measure. It is an invitation to recognize the innate longing for intimacy with God. A longing that has been etched into our very being. We live in a world filled with distractions, and the demands of daily life consume our minds, pulling our hearts in countless directions. However, in the midst of this chaos, we find ourselves yearning for something more. A connection that transcends the superficial and reaches down to the depths of our souls.

King David said in Psalm 63:1–3 (KJV),

O God, thou art my God; early will I seek thee: my soul thirsteth for thee, my flesh longeth for thee in a dry and thirsty land, where no water is; To see thy power and thy glory, so as I have seen thee in the sanctuary. Because thy lovingkindness is better than life, my lips shall praise thee.

How do we respond to this call? How do we embark on this journey toward intimacy with God? It begins with a surrender, relinquishing our desires and ambitions and opening our hearts to God. It requires a willingness to let go of our preconceived notions and expectations to allow God to guide us into the depths of His love.

The apostle Paul, in his letter to the Ephesians, encourages us to be rooted and established in love, [and to] have power, together with all the Lord's holy people, to grasp how wide and long and high and deep is the love of Christ (Ephesians 3:17–18).

These words remind us that intimacy with God is not a shallow endeavor; it is a journey that takes us to the very depths of His love. A love that surpasses our understanding and transforms us from the inside out. As we delve into the pages of this book, we will explore the various facets of intimacy with God. We will uncover the beauty of prayer, the power of worship, the significance of the holy Scripture, and the blessings of communion with the person of the Holy Spirit. We will explore the silence and stillness that allow us to hear God's gentle whispers, and we will discover the joy that comes from surrendering our lives to His divine will.

Through personal stories, reflective insights, and timeless wisdom of the Word of God, we will embark on a transformative journey that calls us to draw closer to the Heavenly Father. It is a journey that requires intentionality, patience, and vulnerability, but the rewards are immeasurable. In developing intimacy with God, we will find the solace our souls crave, the peace that surpasses all understanding, and the abundant love that fills every fiber of our being.

So, dear friend, I invite you to join me on this sacred pilgrimage. Let us heed the call to a deeper relationship with the Heavenly Father, for in Him, we will find the fulfillment our hearts long for. Together, let us uncover the beauty, the joy, and the boundless grace that await us in the intimate embrace of God's love.

CHAPTER 1
THE NATURE OF GOD'S LOVE

"The Lord hath appeared of old unto me, saying, Yea, I have loved thee with an everlasting love: therefore, with lovingkindness have I drawn thee" (Jeremiah 31:3, KJV).

Love is a profound aspect of our existence. It constantly motivates and inspires us. It permeates every aspect of our lives and has the ability to transform us profoundly. Yet, God's love transcends our understanding. The book of 1 John beautifully declares, "God is love" (1 John 4:8, NKJV), encapsulating the fundamental nature of the Almighty. This love flows unconditionally from His heart, extending boundlessly to every corner of creation. The Scriptures unveil the depth of God's love through His deeds and actions. In John 3:16 (NKJV), the Bible declares, "For God so loved the world that he gave his only begotten Son, that whosoever believeth, in him should not perish but have everlasting life." This verse serves as a reminder of the nature of God's boundless affection. It showcases how willingly He offered Jesus Christ as a means to redeem humanity from sin and grant life.

God's love is not based on our worthiness but shines forth even in our brokenness. Romans 5:8 (KJV) reassures us, "But God commendeth his love toward us, in that, while we were yet sinners, Christ died for us." His love pursues us relentlessly, desiring to restore the broken relationship between humanity and the Creator. Also, God's love is all-encompassing and inclusive. First John 4:9 emphasizes that God sent His Son into the world so we might live through Him. This verse reminds us that God's love extends to all people, transcending any barriers and unifying humanity under His divine compassion. As we reflect on the nature of God's love, we comprehend its profound implications for our lives. It offers healing, comfort, and hope. God's love is a refuge where we find solace and rest. It empowers us to love others selflessly, extend grace and forgiveness, and embodies Christ's essence in our interactions with the world.

The Father Is the Initiator

Every experience of love and intimacy we've ever had with the Father (God) always began with His initiation. He started pursuing mankind before the creation of the world, and He initiated pursuit over *you* before you were even born.

"Before I formed you in the womb I knew you, before you were born, I set you apart; I appointed you as a prophet to the nations" (Jeremiah 1:5, NIV).

Our hunger for intimacy isn't something we came up with by ourselves. Rather, it's our response to the invitation that's been there before we were even born. He first stretched His hands and embraced us.

"According as he hath chosen us in him before the foundation of the world, that we should be holy and without blame before him in love" (Ephesians 1:4, KJV).

The magnitude of God's love is beyond measure, and we are invited to experience it intimately. As we surrender to His love, we are transformed, renewed, and set free to live a life rooted in love. It is a love that satisfies our souls, heals our wounds, and empowers us to be vessels of love in a broken world. I want you to always remember this: God's love is sacrificial, unconditional, and all-encompassing. It surpasses human understanding yet beckons us into a personal relationship with our Heavenly Father. Delving deeper into the depths of God's love fulfills our longing and equips us to spread His love in a world that desperately needs it.

Understanding God as a Heavenly Father

When we think of a father, we envision strength, guidance, and unconditional love. A father provides wisdom, protection, and support. Similarly, understanding God as a Heavenly Father surpasses our earthly comprehension and encompasses a depth of love and care. As humans, we long for intimacy with our Creator beyond religious rituals. We desire a personal relationship where God's love embraces and shapes us into our true selves. Isaiah 66:13 portrays God's nurturing nature, comforting us like a mother comforts her child. Like an earthly father, God rejoices in our growth and accomplishments. Zephaniah 3:17 affirms that God rejoices over us with singing, finding delight in our presence, and celebrating our journey of faith. *Every human could flourish and bring forth their best in an atmosphere of love.* God wants to bring the best out of us.

Jesus teaches us to approach God as a loving Father in Matthew 6:9. He invites us to address God with a reverent familiarity, being at ease in His presence, knowing that He longs to hear our prayers and meet our needs.

Understanding God as a Heavenly Father reveals His role as a provider. In Matthew 6:31–32, Jesus assures us that our Heavenly Father knows our needs and cares for us beyond what we can comprehend. We can trust in His provision for our physical, emotional, and spiritual needs. Embracing God as our Heavenly Father transforms our relationship with Him. We approach Him with vulnerability and trust, knowing He listens, understands, and loves without limits. In His presence, we find comfort, security, and unwavering support.

Understanding God as a Heavenly Father transcends theological concepts. It invites us into a deeply personal and transformative experience of His love. I pray for you that your heart will be opened to the depths of His love, allowing His fatherly embrace to shape you into the individual He intended you to be.

The Desire for a Deeper Relationship

Within the depths of our souls lies a profound longing, a deep longing for a connection that transcends the superficialities of life. It is a desire to experience a relationship that reaches into the very core of our being. This desire, this yearning, is the whisper of our souls calling us to seek a deeper relationship with our Heavenly Father. As human beings, we are wired for relationships and connection. We are not created to be loners. We crave intimacy and long to be known, seen, and understood. This desire is woven into the fabric of our existence, compelling us to seek relationships that go beyond surface-level interactions. And yet, as we journey through life, we discover that our deepest longings cannot be fully satisfied by human relationships alone. There is a longing within us—a yearning that can only find fulfillment in a relationship with our Creator.

This desire for a deeper relationship emerges in moments of quiet reflection in the midst of life's trials and triumphs. It arouses within us when we witness the beauty of nature or experience moments of profound joy or sorrow. It is a longing that cannot be silenced, an invitation to delve into the depths of our souls and explore the mysteries of our existence. We were made for communion—with God and with one another. The Scriptures echo this truth, reminding us that we were created in the image of God and designed for relationship. In the book of Genesis, it is written, "And God said, Let us make man in our image, after our likeness" (Genesis 1:26, KJV). This foundational truth reveals that at our core, we bear the imprint of our Heavenly Father, and our souls yearn for a connection with our Maker.

Therefore, as we explore the pages of the Bible, we encounter stories of individuals who sought a deeper relationship with God. We witness the psalmist pouring out his heart in prayer, seeking solace and understanding. We find prophets wrestling with doubts and fears yet ultimately surrendering to God's mysterious ways. These stories serve as signposts, guiding us on our own journey of seeking a deeper relationship with the Heavenly Father. *The desire for a deeper relationship is not a call to embark on a solitary quest. It is an invitation to draw near to the Father and to walk alongside fellow seekers.* It is an opportunity to cultivate an authentic community where we can learn from one another, encourage one another, and experience the transformative power of shared spiritual growth. As we gather together, we discover that the desire for a deeper relationship is not confined to our individual hearts but is a collective longing that unites us as spiritual beings on a shared path.

Embracing the desire for a deeper relationship requires vulnerability—a willingness to submit ourselves fully to the working grace of God. It calls us to lay down our pretenses, our doubts, and our fears and surrender to the vastness of God's love. It beckons on us to let go of our self-reliance and trust that in our vulnerability, we will encounter the boundless grace of our Heavenly Father. In the depths of our souls, we hear the call to embark on a journey towards a deeper relationship with God. It is a journey that requires intentionality, perseverance, and a willingness to be transformed. It is a journey that invites us to explore the mysteries of our existence, to wrestle with questions that have no easy answers, and to surrender to the profound love that waits patiently for us.

I pray that we heed the call of our hearts and souls to embark on this sacred pilgrimage—a journey that leads us to the depths of who we are created to be and into the arms of a loving Father, our Creator. As we step into the unknown, we find solace, purpose, and fulfillment beyond measure. This journey may appear as uncharted territory to our physical being, but it is familiar to our spirit because the presence of God is our natural habitat. It is where we emanate from, where we truly come alive. May our desire for a deeper relationship with God guide our steps, awaken our hearts, and lead us ever closer to our Heavenly Father.

CHAPTER 2
LONGING FOR THE FATHER'S EMBRACE

Losing a parent is an experience that leaves an indelible mark on one's life, especially when it happens during the formative years. As a little boy, I faced the devastating loss of my loving father. My dad was a hardworking man who devoted his daytime to farming and worked as a security guard at night. Though his time with us was limited to primarily weekends, every moment we spent together was etched into my memories. His unwavering love for our family and his passion for music shaped my life in profound ways.

Though my dad was only with us on the weekends, those precious moments that we spent together were filled with love and joy. Saturday and Sunday mornings were greeted by his music, which became a cherished family tradition. The melodies he played filled our home, uplifting our spirits and creating a sense of togetherness. Even in the brief time we had, he made every moment count.

His commitment to hard work was unparalleled. Balancing his responsibilities as a farmer and a security guard demanded tremendous dedication and sacrifice. Despite the long hours and physical labor, he never complained. His strong work ethic became a guiding principle in our family, instilling values of perseverance and determination into most of his children. His death left a vacuum in our home that no one else could fill. It was a lot of struggle for my mother and the rest of the family. I looked up to various people to fill this void in my life, but it never worked. No one could fill his shoes in my life. The more I looked, the more disappointed I felt. There is no man that could replace the love of my father in my heart. There is a compassion and care that could only be found in the heart of a good father. At that point in my life, I felt hopeless and lonely, thinking I would never experience such love again. Unknown to me that there is another Father whose love is greater and eternal.

Meeting My Heavenly Father

It was a chilly morning in the early months of 1990 when, as a teenager, I made a life-changing decision. Although I had been a member of the church for quite some time, I only attended church as part of a family tradition. It was more of a social gathering and a place to hang out with my friends. After years of wrestling with my faith, I finally surrendered to the invitation to be reconciled with my Heavenly Father. This encounter marked a pivotal point in my spiritual journey.

As I stood before the altar, tears streaming down my face, I felt a weight lifting off my shoulders. It was as if a burden of guilt and shame was being replaced by a sense of peace and restoration. I knew at that instant that my life would never be the same again.

Embracing my newfound relationship with God, I delved into His Word, eager to understand His heart and His plans for my life. I took everything I read in the Bible literally. In fact, I was so expectant to the point that I thought, like Jesus, a physical dove would rest on my head during my water baptism. I wanted everything that Jesus had. I wanted an experience like His. His love and grace became my daily bread, sustaining me through the ups and downs of life. I soon realized that there was more to my faith than simply being born again. There had to be more.

Driven by Hunger

Driven by a hunger for deeper spiritual experiences, I sought to understand and experience the power of the Holy Spirit. It was through this pursuit that I entered into a whole new realm of adventure. Just a few months after my reconciliation with God, I received the baptism of the Holy Spirit. This electrifying encounter was a catalyst for a series of extraordinary events that revealed the depth of God's love and power.

The baptism of the Holy Spirit brought forth a divine empowerment that I had never known before. It was as if a fire had been ignited within me, propelling me towards a newfound purpose and calling. I began to experience the presence and guidance of the Holy Spirit in my everyday life, leading me to opportunities I had never imagined.

Sharing My Story

With each passing day, the power of God unfolded in my life. I witnessed miracles, both big and small, as God orchestrated divine connections and interventions. As I shared my testimony with others, I saw lives transformed and hearts awakened to the reality of God's love. It was in these moments that I realized the immense impact that sharing our personal stories has on shaping the lives of those around us.

In the midst of our individual journey, we often underestimate the power of recounting our stories. Yet, it is through our personal struggles, triumphs, and encounters with God that we have the ability to inspire and encourage others. Each one of us has a unique narrative crafted by the hand of God, and it is through the telling of our stories that His redemptive power is unleashed as we encourage and sharpen one another.

When we share our stories and what the cross of Christ has done in our lives, we create a space for vulnerability, authenticity, and healing. As we unveil the chapters of our lives, we invite others to do the same, fostering a sense of camaraderie and understanding. It is through the unity of our stories that we can truly experience the transformative power of God in our churches.

So, let us not shy away from our stories. Let us embrace the power they hold and the potential they possess. Whether through written words, spoken words, singing, or acts of kindness, let us use our stories to inspire, encourage, and bring hope to a world desperately in need.

As I reflect on my own journey, I am humbled by the realization that meeting my Heavenly Father was the greatest thing that ever happened to me. Through the ensuing chapters of my life, I have come to understand His unwavering love.

"But God demonstrates his own love for us in this: While we were still sinners, Christ died for us" (Romans 5:8, NIV).

CHAPTER 3
THE BIBLE AS A BOOK OF LOVE AND REDEMPTION

As followers of Christ Jesus, we experience the overflowing love of God in our hearts (Romans 5:5). The Bible tells a captivating story that revolves around themes of love and redemption. It goes beyond being a collection of events or moral teachings; rather, it speaks to the deepest desires of our human souls. It reveals the pursuit of love and the limitless grace of a God who desires to redeem and renew humanity.

When we immerse ourselves in the Scriptures, we encounter a God whose love knows no bounds. This love extends to those who are broken, lost, and marginalized. It reaches into the depths of despair and offers hope. Throughout the Old Testament, we catch glimpses of this love—a love that chose Abraham and his descendants, a love that rescued the Israelites from slavery in Egypt, and a love that sustained them during their wilderness journey. However, the ultimate expression of God's compassion and redemption can be found in the New Testament.

The birth of Jesus Christ, the Son of God, inaugurates a new era—a divine intervention in human history. Jesus becomes the personification of God's love and the ultimate agent of redemption through His life, teachings, and sacrificial death.

The Gospels unveil the story of Jesus—a story of compassion, forgiveness, and radical love. Jesus, in His interactions with the outcasts, the sinners, and the broken, demonstrates a love that defies societal norms and embraces all. He dines with tax collectors, heals the sick, and offers forgiveness to those burdened by guilt. His life becomes a testament to the transformative power of love and the redemptive work that God longs to accomplish in each of our lives. The crucifixion and resurrection of Jesus Christ represent the apex of this story of compassion and redemption. On the cross, Jesus voluntarily absorbs the crimes of humanity and offers himself as the perfect sacrifice. He who knew no sin became sin for us (2 Corinthians 5:21). It is through His death and resurrection that the depths of God's love and the magnitude of His redemptive plan are revealed. As the apostle Paul declares in Ephesians 1:4 (NIV), "For he chose us in him before the creation of the world to be holy and blameless in his sight. In love."

You Have a Role to Play

The Bible not only tells a story of love and redemption but invites us to participate in it. It calls us to respond to God's love, accept His redemptive work in our lives, and embrace the transformative power of His grace. It challenges us to love our neighbors, extend forgiveness, and embody the very essence of God's love in our interactions with the world. In the pages of the Bible, we find comfort in times of sorrow, guidance in moments of uncertainty, and hope in the face of adversity. It is a book that speaks to the human experience at all levels, acknowledging our struggles, doubts, and brokenness while pointing us toward the redemptive love of God. It is a book that reminds us that we are not alone and that in the midst of our pain, there is a God who loves us unconditionally and seeks to redeem and restore our lives.

As we engage with the Bible, may we approach it not merely as a book of rules or intellectual pursuits but as a sacred text that reveals the depths of God's love and the transformative power of redemption. May it inspire us to live lives of love, compassion, and grace as we embrace the story of love and redemption that unfolds within its pages.

Exploring God's Relationship with His Children Throughout the Scripture

Throughout the pages of the Scriptures, we are invited to explore the multifaceted relationship between God and His children. It is a relationship that spans time, cultures, and generations—a relationship marked by love, faithfulness, and unwavering commitment. As we delve into the stories and teachings found within the Bible, we witness the intricate tapestry of this divinity-humanity connection.

Before time ever began, I mean from the very beginning, we see glimpses of God's desire for an intimate relationship with His children. In the book of Genesis, we encounter the narrative of Adam and Eve, where God walks with them in the cool of the day and delights in their company. However, as the story unfolds, we witness the tragic rupture caused by sin—a rupture that necessitates the redemptive work of God throughout history. As we journey through the Old Testament, we witness the unfolding drama of God's relationship with His chosen people, Israel. Through prophets, priests, and kings, God reveals His character,

His promises, and His unfailing love. We see Him leading the Israelites out of slavery in Egypt, guiding them through the wilderness, and establishing them as a nation in the promised land. Despite their constant rebellion and faithlessness, God remains steadfast, always seeking to reconcile and restore His relationship with His wayward children.

The Psalms, often considered the emotional heart of the Bible, provide us with a window into the deep longing for communion with God. The psalmists pour out their hearts in prayers, laments, and songs of praise, expressing their yearning to dwell in the presence of the Almighty. Their words resonate with the joys and sorrows of the human experience, offering us a glimpse of the profound connection between God and His children.

In the New Testament, we witness the climax of God's redemptive plan through the person of Jesus Christ. In the life, teachings, death, and resurrection of Jesus, we see the ultimate revelation of God's love for His children. Jesus refers to His followers as His friends (John 15:15), and He invites them into a relationship characterized by trust, love, and obedience. He teaches them to address God as "Our Father" (Matthew 6:9, NIV), emphasizing the familial nature of the bond between God and His children. Through Jesus, we also receive the gift of the Holy Spirit, who dwells within believers, guiding, comforting, and empowering them. The Holy Spirit deepens our relationship with God, enabling us to cry out "Abba, Father" (Romans 8:15, NIV) and experience a profound sense of adoption as God's children (Galatians 4:4–7). Through the Holy Spirit, we are united with Christ and become partakers of the divine nature (2 Peter 1:4).

The apostle Paul beautifully describes the inseparable love between God and His children in Romans 8:38–39 (KJV), stating, "For I am persuaded, that neither death, nor life, nor angels, nor principalities, nor powers, nor things present, nor things to come, nor height, nor depth, nor any other creature, shall be able to separate us from the love of God, which is in Christ Jesus our Lord."

As we explore God's relationship with His children throughout the Scripture, we discover a love that surpasses human comprehension—a love that is constant, faithful, and unchanging. It is a love that seeks us out in our brokenness, forgives our shortcomings, and offers us a pathway to restoration. It is a love that uncovers and heals every hidden hurt generated by offenses and disappointments. It is a love that invites us to know Him intimately, to walk in His ways, and to live as His beloved children.

My earnest, heartfelt prayer for you as you read this book is that as you go through this exploration of God's relationship with His children, the believers in Christ Jesus, may it deepen your understanding of His love, strengthen your faith, and inspire you to walk in the fullness of your identity as His cherished sons and daughters.

Recognizing the Father's Love and Redemption Plan

In our human journey, there are times when we feel lost, broken, and burdened by the weight of our mistakes and failures. We yearn for a love that sees beyond our flaws, a love that offers redemption and restoration. In those moments, we are invited to recognize the Father's love and His incredible redemption plan woven throughout history. The Father's love is unlike any other love we may encounter in this world. It is a love that knows us intimately, a love that sees the depths of our hearts and accepts us just as we are. It is a love that embraces us in our brokenness and whispers words of forgiveness and healing. It is a love that sees the best in us. It is a love that sees us as gold in a raw state and willing to bring the best out of it. It is a love that offers hope and extends an invitation to partake in His redemption plan.

The story of redemption begins in the Garden of Eden, where the first humans, Adam and Eve, rebelled against God and introduced sin into the world. In that moment, the Father's heart was filled with sorrow, yet even then, He set in motion a plan to restore what was broken. He promised a Savior who would come to reconcile humanity to Himself. Throughout the pages of Scripture, we witness the unfolding of this redemption plan. The Old Testament is replete with prophecies, promises, and foreshadowing of the coming Messiah. From the prophetic words of Isaiah to the sacrificial system established in Leviticus, we see glimpses of the Father's love and His longing to bring His children back into a right relationship with Him.

Then, in the fullness of time, the Father sent His Son, Jesus Christ, into the world. Jesus, the embodiment of the Father's love, came to live among us to reveal the Father's heart and to accomplish the work of redemption. Through His teachings, miracles, and ultimately, His sacrificial death on the cross, Jesus demonstrated the Father's love in its purest form. It is through Jesus that we come to fully recognize the depth of the Father's love and the extent of His redemption plan. In Ephesians 1:7 (KJV), the apostle Paul proclaims, "In whom [Jesus] we have redemption through his blood, the forgiveness of sins, according to the riches of his grace."[1] Through His sacrifice, Jesus paid the price for our sins and provided a way for us to be reconciled to the Father.

Recognizing the Father's love and redemption plan is not merely an intellectual understanding. It is a personal encounter with grace and mercy. It is how we come to the realization that we are undeserving of His love, yet He loves us unconditionally. When we recognize this love, we experience His forgiveness and feel the weight of guilt and shame lifted from our shoulders. It enables us to grasp the truth that through Jesus, we have been redeemed and made new. In recognizing the Father's love and redemption plan, we also embrace our role in this grand narrative. As recipients of His love and grace, we are called to extend that love and grace to others. Just as the Father has redeemed us, He invites us to participate in His work of redemption in the lives of those around us. We become vessels of His love, agents of His grace, and ambassadors of His redemption plan according to 2 Corinthians 5:19b.

May our hearts be awakened to the Father's love that pursues us, forgives us, and transforms us. May we recognize His redemption plan that offers hope and restoration. And may we have the capacity to embrace the love and, in turn, extend that love and redemption to a world in need, knowing that we are partnering with the Father in His eternal work of reconciling all things to Himself. In recognizing the Father's love and His redemption plan, we find solace, purpose, and unshakable hope. It is this

---

1. Word in parenthesis added by the author.

recognition that brings us into a deeper relationship with Him. A relationship characterized by gratitude, surrender, and unyielding trust in His boundless love.

CHAPTER 4
RESPONDING TO GOD'S LOVE

One of the captivating aspects of God's love is its comprehensive nature. It goes beyond race, gender, and social status. At the heart of God's love lies a desire for a connection with humanity. This love doesn't just bring us closer to God so we can remain unchanged; it transforms our lives. It is a love that transcends our comprehension beyond our flaws and weaknesses and stretches far beyond our earthly existence.

It is a love that seeks to heal, restore, and guide us towards a greater and purposeful life.

However, despite this universality, not everyone responds to the invitation of God's love. Some may turn a blind eye, consumed by their own selfish desires and pursuits. Others may be unable to see beyond their own pain and suffering or fathom a love that is so all-encompassing. Still, others may be burdened by doubt and skepticism, questioning the existence of such a love in a world scarred by selfishness, injustice, and suffering.

Paul's prayer for the Ephesians:

For this reason I bow my knees to the Father of our Lord Jesus Christ, from whom the whole family in heaven and earth is named, that He would grant you, according to the riches of His glory, to be strengthened with might through

His Spirit in the inner man, that Christ may dwell in your hearts through faith; that you, being rooted and grounded in love, may be able to comprehend with all the saints what is the width and length and depth and height— to know the love of Christ which passes knowledge; that you may be filled with all the fullness of God.

Ephesians 3:14–19 (NKJV)

To many people in our generation, it is hard to comprehend how such love still exists. Many view God's love as conditional, believing they are unworthy of such a divine affection. In a world driven by materialism and instant gratification, the pursuit of worldly pleasures often overshadows the search for spiritual enlightenment. The noise of social media, consumerism, and the relentless pursuit of success can drown out the still, small voice of God's love, leaving individuals spiritually adrift and unsatisfied. Past mistakes, feelings of guilt and shame, or a distorted self-image can lead individuals to believe that they are undeserving of God's love. As a result, they distance themselves from this love, shutting themselves off from the healing power and transformative grace that could help them overcome their struggles.

A Profound Story of Unconditional Love

The timeless parable of the prodigal son has captivated readers and learners for centuries, unraveling invaluable insights into the nature of forgiveness, repentance, and the boundless love of a father. This profound story, recounted in the biblical Gospel of Luke, depicts a father's unwavering love towards his wayward son and echoes a universal truth that transcends religious boundaries and resonates with readers of all backgrounds. With its timeless message, the prodigal son's story continues to inspire seekers of wisdom and serve as a guiding light in a world hungering for compassion and acceptance.

At the heart of this parable lies the figure of the prodigal son, a young man who asks his father for his inheritance prematurely, abandoning his family and squandering his riches in a distant land. Overtaken by his recklessness and prodigal extravagance, the son finds himself broken and destitute at the nadir of his existence. This moral fallacy illuminates the universal human propensity to err, to be lured by temptations, and to lose oneself in the pursuit of transient pleasures.

Despite the son's transgressions, the most poignant aspect of this story is the father's unwavering love for his wayward child. When the prodigal son, reduced to penury, returns home, he is greeted not with disdain or reproach but with open arms and genuine joy. This father's love surpasses all understanding, for rather than condemning his son's past actions or demanding retribution, he embraces him and throws a grand celebration to mark his return.

This parable acts as a mirror of the human condition. As flawed beings, we all experience moments of waywardness and shortcomings, leaving us feeling lost and estranged. This story serves as a powerful reminder that, regardless of our failures or missteps, there is always hope for redemption and reconciliation with love, both human and divine.

A Call to Action

In Luke 15:18, The prodigal son made up his mind to go back to his father. He decided to take action. "I will arise and go to my father, and will say to him, "Father, I have sinned against heaven and before you" (Luke 15:18, NKJV).

The invitation to respond to God's love is not a passive one. It calls for action, for a conscious decision to open our hearts and minds to the transformative power of this love. It requires us to seek answers to long-standing questions lying in the depths of our souls, constantly tugging at our hearts. To question the thoughts that remind us of our inadequacies, making us hesitant to accept this great love. And to wrestle with and overcome our doubts and fears about the authenticity of such a pure love being freely extended towards us yet asking for nothing more than for the invitation to be accepted by faith. It compels us to love not only those who are easy to love but also those who challenge us, testing the boundaries of our patience and compassion.

For those who have fallen from under the grace and are carrying the weight of past failures, it can be difficult to believe that God could ever love you again. You may think that you have exhausted your chances, that there is no way back to the loving arms of the Heavenly Father. You may find yourselves in situations where it seems like there is no way out. You made mistakes, you fell short, and you feel like you have disappointed not only yourself but also those around you and blew it big with God. The enemy wants you to believe that your case is beyond redemption. It is in these moments of despair and hopelessness that God's unfailing love and grace shine through. He is a God of more than a second chance. His love knows no bounds. He is always ready to welcome us back into His embrace. There is hope. The father has not given up on you. You must respond to His call at this moment.

In responding to God's love, we become vessels of grace, extending love and kindness to the world around us. If we want love in our world, in the churches, and in our families, we must first respond to God's love. In responding to this love, we become agents of change, working towards justice and reconciliation. We become bearers of hope, offering solace to those who grieve and strength to those who falter. Through our response to God's love, we become instruments of divine love in a world desperately in need of healing and renewal.

Unmasking the Enemy's Scheme

When the father joyously welcomed his prodigal son home and threw a celebration to mark the occasion, the older brother felt a surge of jealousy. This raw emotion highlights the universal struggle humans face when comparing themselves with others, which often leads to bitterness and resentment. We want people to suffer for the evil they did to us. This is different from seeking justice in the court of law. Many have become sick under the weight of bitterness and revenge. Today, many sermons from the pulpit are polluted and tainted with bitterness and unforgiveness from the preacher's past experience.

The older brother's emotional turmoil serves as a reminder that jealousy can cloud our judgment, preventing us from seeing through the lens through which God sees His children.

The prodigal son's brother became consumed by jealousy and self-centeredness, focusing solely on his own sacrifices and feeling deprived when his brother returned home to a joyous celebration. He couldn't comprehend the actions of his father toward his brother. He questioned the generosity and the judgment of their father toward his brother. From a human's perspective, what the father did was not fair. That is the reason why the Bible says that the *ways of God are not the ways of men* (Isaiah 55:8). Had the prodigal son encountered his disheartened brother first, the chances of successfully reaching their father's loving embrace may have been lost. The prodigal son's brother thought that he could buy his way to his father's heart through services. There are well-known believers who erroneously think that they have better chances with God based on the services they render in the kingdom. They wrongly assume that the higher their service to God, the more of the love of God they'll experience. Although God rewards diligence, His love for each one of His children is complete and unwavering. It does not fluctuate. No act of service will make Him love us more than He already does. He paid the same price for all. The same blood was shed once and for all.

> For you are all sons of God through faith in Christ Jesus. For as many of you as were baptized into Christ have put on Christ. There is neither Jew nor Greek, there is neither slave nor free, there is neither male nor female; for you are all one in Christ Jesus. And if you are Christ's, then you are Abraham's seed, and heirs according to the promise.
>
> Galatians 3:26–29 (NKJV)

In today's society, where success is often measured by material possessions and external achievements, it is easy to lose sight of our own self-worth and fall into the trap of comparison.

The enemy has blinded many to the unconditional love of the Father. On the surface, they smile at you, but deep down, the feelings of rivalry and judgmental attitude towards others' success are eating up their souls. The mere thought of someone else's success would trigger feelings of deprivation within them. It is as though the other person's breakthrough decreases their own chances of experiencing such success. They find it hard to celebrate and rejoice with those who rejoice. Unknown to them, they are disqualifying themselves from experiencing such joy. They are like the prodigal son's brother whose focus is on himself. Instead of embracing his brother and joining in the celebration, he distanced himself, consumed by his anger and resentment. In this pivotal part of the story, we see the importance of compassion and forgiveness. It encourages us to let go of our grievances, extending forgiveness even when it seems undeserved. By doing so, we can break the cycle of resentment and create an atmosphere of love and understanding. We also free ourselves to enjoy the riches of the Father's blessings. He is not a respecter of persons. He can do in your life what you see Him do for others. Sadly, the prodigal son's brother has been oblivious to the fact that he had free access to everything that the Father had all along. He didn't know that celebrating his brother's return was not a threat to his own chances of having a party thrown in his honor if he so desired. Cultivating a heart that seeks the Father's love above personal achievements opens the door to genuine compassion for others. By consciously choosing to embrace the truth that the Father's love is immeasurable and without conditions, individuals can develop an unshakeable foundation of love, leading to greater fulfillment and spiritual growth.

God's love is an all-encompassing force that beckons all humans to embrace its transformative power. At its core, responding to God's love requires a willingness to let go, relinquish control, and open oneself up to the ineffable grace and mercy that God offers. It may be daunting, but it holds the promise of a life filled with purpose, joy, and ultimate fulfillment. May we all have the courage to accept God's invitation and experience the immeasurable depth of His love.

CHAPTER 5
TRUE IDENTITY COMES FROM THE FATHER

Growing up as a fatherless child, I struggled with the issue of acceptance. From a young age, I yearned to be liked, to fit in, and to gain the approval of those around me. This struggle with acceptance shaped my character and influenced my behavior, leading me toward a relentless pursuit of pleasing others.

In my quest for acceptance, I developed various strategies to win the favor of those I encountered. I observed how different people responded positively to different actions and words, and I carefully adapted my behavior accordingly. It became a difficult balancing act as I tried to conform to the expectations of others, constantly striving to be someone they would approve of.

However, this effort to please everyone proved to be both physically and emotionally draining. I soon realized that it was impossible to satisfy everyone's expectations. Many individuals took advantage of my vulnerability and exploited my desire for acceptance as I desperately attempted to fit into different molds. I became an easy target, constantly bending over backward to meet others' demands.

This struggle with acceptance had a profound impact on my self-esteem. The constant rejection and disappointment left me feeling inadequate and unworthy. I began to question my own values, believing that I needed to constantly prove myself to others to be accepted and validated. On the other hand, not having a confidant in those days was a great advantage, although it did not feel like it at the time. I later realized how much that period of my life shaped my personal relationship with the Holy Spirit. He became my friend and confidant. I could talk to Him without feeling judged or unworthy. I appreciated His friendship deeply because it helped me in the place of prayer and communion with the Father. I longed to be in His presence daily as He took me on a journey of self-discovery. Those were times of reunion with my true self. Sometimes, I would cry all night, praising God for such a love as His.

As I journeyed with Him, I gradually came to understand that true acceptance does not come from pleasing others but from seeing and loving myself the way God does. I realized that I had been prioritizing the desires and opinions of others over God's opinions and approval over my life. This is true for many people in our world today.

This newfound understanding empowered me to reevaluate my relationships. I learned the importance of discerning the opinions, intentions, and expectations of others. I found that not everyone's acceptance is worth pursuing, especially if it comes at the cost of sacrificing your identity and losing yourself in the process. I discovered the power of confidently asserting my personal values and convictions at the risk of facing disapproval from others. True acceptance comes from within, and it is far more valuable than the fleeting approval of others. This is such a liberating truth for me.

What your creator says about you should be the final. He is the only one who knows your true value. As the monetary value in hand must be equal to the value of the item being purchased, God gave the blood of His only Son, Jesus Christ, in exchange for your redemption. Jesus took your place. He was the perfect substitute (1 Corinthians 6:20). To God, that is your worth—life for life. Your life is that much valuable to your Heavenly Father. Hallelujah!

My heart aches when I see people struggling with acceptance and validation. I can feel their pain because I was once in their shoes. In today's fast-paced and ever-changing world, the issue of identity has become a pressing concern for many individuals, particularly among the younger generation. As technology advances and societal norms continue to shift, young people find themselves grappling with the fundamental question of who they are and how they fit into the world around them. This struggle with identity has profound implications on various aspects of their lives, including relationships, career choices, mental health, spirituality, and overall well-being.

Studies demonstrate that those with low self-esteem are more likely to experience anxiety, despair, and loneliness. Young people's mental health can worsen due to peer pressure and the fear of being different. Lack of a consistent self-identity may also make it hard to form meaningful interactions and relationships. Social media exposure is a major cause of this generation's identity dilemma. Social media can be a great tool for connection and self-expression, but it can also lead to unhealthy comparisons and feelings of inadequacy. Young people are bombarded with carefully managed images of success and happiness, which can cause worry, self-doubt, and self-perception distortion. As they try to fit into social media's model, people may lose sight of their actual values and objectives, making it harder to find themselves.

Society tells us that our worth is determined by our achievements, possessions, appearance, etc. We are encouraged to chase after success, popularity, and material wealth. Some ministers of the Gospel are constantly measuring and comparing themselves with other ministers. They aspire for positions and visibilities. They fight for it, quarrel over it, and abuse others in the process. But deep down, we know there must be more to life than this superficial pursuit of happiness. We long for something greater, something that gives our lives meaning and purpose. And that is where our true identity can only be found—in God.

We discover that we are not defined by our accomplishments or failures but by the fact that we are created in the image of God. We are His beloved children; our true worth lies in our relationship with Him. It is in this relationship that we find our true purpose and identity. When we allow God to define our identity, we find that our worth is not based on our appearance or our achievements but on the value placed on us by the One who formed us. We discover that true beauty comes from within, in godly character and the ability to love God and serve others, stemming from a pure heart. We realize that our purpose is not to pursue selfish desires but to live and serve the purpose of God for our generation (Ephesians 2:10).

When we find our true identity in God, we can break free from every societal pressure to be better, do better, and have more. We become free from the rat race fueled by comparison and perfectionism. We'll no longer need to measure ourselves against others or strive for an unattainable standard of success. Instead, we can find contentment and fulfillment in who we are in God.

Finding our identity in God also brings a sense of peace and security. When we know that our worth is not dependent on the vacillating opinions of others or our own performance, we can relinquish the perpetual desire for recognition and approval. We can rest in the knowledge that we are deeply loved and fully accepted by our Creator, regardless of our imperfections and shortcomings.

However, finding our identity in God is not a one-time event. We must remain in God.

"I am the vine; you are the branches. If you remain in me and I in you, you will bear much fruit; apart from me you can do nothing" (John 15:5, NIV). Finding our identity in God is an ongoing journey of self-discovery and growth. It requires daily surrendering to God, fellowshipping with the Holy Spirit, and seeking His guidance and wisdom. It means allowing Him to shape and mold us into the people He created us to be. It starts with spending time in His presence, praying, meditating, and studying His Word. It means surrounding ourselves with a community of believers who can encourage and support us on our spiritual journey. And it means staying open to the promptings of the Holy Spirit and trusting God to lead us in the right direction. Finding our identity in God is a revolutionary act that leads to self-acceptance, as God loves us in a world that tells us we have to be someone else to be accepted. It is a reminder that with His approval over our lives, we are enough just as we are, and our true worth lies in our relationship with our Creator (2 Corinthians 10:18). So let us embrace our true identity in God and live our lives with purpose, passion, and authenticity. May God help you in this journey of discovery.

CHAPTER 6
MOVING BEYOND RULES AND REGULATIONS: LEGALISM VS. GRACE

As human beings, we often feel constrained by rules and societal expectations. These external standards shape our behavior and mindset, but we yearn for a more authentic and meaningful way of living. Moving beyond rules and regulations begins with the realization that our worth as human beings is not defined by external standards. We are not mere products of societal expectations but unique individuals with unique values, beliefs, and desires. The awareness of these grants individuals the ability to liberate themselves from the constraints of societal norms and embrace their authentic identities.

Christianity is beyond a set of dos and don'ts. It is a dynamic life that streams from the power of the Holy Spirit. In some cases, following rules and regulations creates only behavioral modification without genuine transformation from the heart. An individual can modify their behavior to meet the perceived expectation when other believers are around in order to gain the approval of others. This leads to a life of pretense and hypocrisy, a life that is void of authenticity and integrity. Such a person may gain the approval of men but not that of God because God looks beyond the outward appearance (1 Samuel 16:7).

When misused, rules and regulations become carnally motivated restrictions and, like prison bars, limit our growth and potential.

This is in no way a disregard for structure and discipline or the authority that God has placed over us. Instead, rules and regulations should serve as guidelines and tools to aid us in living our best lives.

Law vs. Grace

"Christ is become of no effect unto you, whosoever of you are justified by the law; ye are fallen from grace" (Galatians 5:4, KJV).

In essence, the law is based on the principles of fairness and justice. Its mission was to guide and govern human conduct by setting boundaries and demanding accountability. Despite its intended goals, the law unavoidably reveals our human limits and frailties. In our greatest efforts, we consistently fall short of its ideal norms and righteous requirements. Thus, at its best, the law only serves to remind us of our sinful nature and the impossibility of achieving genuine righteousness by our own efforts. It cannot bring us closer to God on its own.

In recognizing the law's inability to bridge the gap between humanity and a holy God, an alternative solution emerges. Its inadequacies brought to bear the need for a divine intervention. The need for a manifestation of God's love and mercy becomes evident, for without the rightful intervention, humans would remain in a state of perpetual separation from their creator— forever grasping for a connection that seemed unattainable to any human.

Jesus the Way, the Truth, and the Life

With the arrival of Jesus, the long-awaited Messiah, a profound shift occurred in the relationship between humanity and God. Jesus, the Son of God, is His personified divine love, compassion, and sacrifice. Through His teachings, miracles, and ultimately, His death and resurrection, Jesus brought us closer to the Father. He paved the way for a new covenant that transcends the limitations of the law.

Jesus became the ultimate mediator between man and God. He reconciled humanity to God by bearing the weight of our sins on the cross. His sacrificial act offered both redemption and forgiveness, eradicating the insurmountable distance sin had created between man and God. He removed the gap that the law was unable to fill. He became the fulfillment of the law (Matthew 5:17; Romans 8:3–4). When we place our faith in Jesus, we are granted access to the Father, finding solace and guidance on our spiritual journey. Jesus brought us closer to the Father by showing us the true nature of God's love. He taught us that salvation is not found through a rigid adherence to religious laws but through a personal relationship with God. He demonstrated this through His own life and ministry.

Throughout His ministry, Jesus interacted with people from all walks of life—the outcasts, the sinners, and the marginalized. He offered them forgiveness and acceptance, showing them that God's love was not based on their ability to keep the law. He met them as sinners but didn't leave them in their sinful state. Their lives were transformed as they turned from their sin to become His followers. It was this radical inclusion that enabled those who were alienated from God to draw near to him. Those who were otherwise alienated from God's covenant (Colossians 1:21–23).

Furthermore, Jesus emphasized the importance of grace over legalism. He challenged the religious leaders of His time, pointing out their hypocrisy and the oppressive burden of rules they placed on the people. He taught that it is by God's grace alone that we are saved, not by our own works or our efforts to keep the law. In contrast to the law, Jesus offers us a relationship with God that is based on love, grace, and mercy. He invites us to find solace in God's embrace, to seek forgiveness, acceptance, and renewal, and to experience a closeness to our Creator that the law could never provide.

Removing the Veil

The veil is a symbolic representation of separation and division. In ancient times, the veil was a physical barrier in the Jewish temple that separated the Holy of Holies, where God was believed to dwell, from the rest of the temple. It signified the inaccessibility of God to ordinary people. Only the high priest could enter this innermost sanctuary once a year, even then, with great caution. However, Jesus, through His life, death, and resurrection, brought about a profound shift in this arrangement. In the Gospel of Matthew, at the moment of Jesus' death, the veil in the temple was torn in two from top to bottom, signifying the end of the separation between God and humanity (Matthew 27:51). This powerful occurrence portrays Jesus as the bridge that connects us to the Father, breaking down the barriers and granting us direct access to our Father, God. With the veil torn, we are liberated from the need for religious rituals, intermediary figures, or elaborate ceremonies to approach God. Jesus' sacrifice paved the way for a new relationship with God, a relationship that is based on freedom, vulnerability, and authenticity. We no longer need to hide behind masks or pretend to be someone we are not. We can come before God as we truly are, with all our strengths, weaknesses, doubts, and imperfections! This newfound freedom extends beyond any established religious structures. It permeates all aspects of our lives, shaping our relationships and self-perception and bringing us to a place of peace that surpasses all understanding. Jesus' teachings emphasize the importance of authenticity and genuine connection. He encourages us to love our neighbors as ourselves, to forgive others as we have been forgiven, and to embrace humility and compassion.

By taking away the veil, Jesus provides us with the opportunity to experience a deep sense of personal liberation. We are invited to shed the chains of fear, shame, and judgment and step into a realm of love, acceptance, and grace. We no longer need to measure our worth based on external criteria or conform to societal expectations. Instead, we can find solace in the knowledge that we are unconditionally loved by our Heavenly Father. Nevertheless, embracing this freedom requires a willingness to let go of our own pretenses and ego-driven desires. It calls for a radical transformation of the self as we learn to relinquish control and surrender to God's will. This means confronting our insecurities, facing painful truths, and releasing old patterns that no longer serve us. When we remove the veils of pretense and allow our authentic selves to shine forth, we create the space for a genuine connection with God and others. Jesus' teachings emphasize the importance of authenticity and genuine connection. He encourages us to love our neighbors as ourselves, to forgive others as we have been forgiven, and to embrace humility and compassion.

Take Off Your Own Veil

Even though God has removed the veil, many Christians are still held back by their own veil. They are covered with the veil of facade and pretense. They come to God pretentiously, forgetting that they are dealing with the same One who formed their inward parts and knows all about them (Psalm 139:13–16). Moving beyond rules and regulations requires us to live with integrity. Integrity entails being true to oneself, even when it is challenging or unpopular. It means you are not living a double life. Your secret and public life are in sync. You are not saying one thing while your action is saying something else. It is about consistently acting in accordance with our values and principles regardless of external pressures or expectations. When we live with integrity, we can navigate through life with a sense of purpose and authenticity.

CHAPTER 7
EMBRACING RELATIONSHIP OVER LEGALISM

As human beings, we have a natural inclination towards seeking connection and a sense of belonging. We long for relationships rooted in love, acceptance, and understanding. However, there are times when our pursuit of connection can become overshadowed by a tendency towards legalism—a rigid adherence to rules, regulations, and external expectations. To experience true and meaningful relationships, we must shift our focus from legalism to embracing the beauty of genuine connection. Relating with God should not be based on keeping a set of rules but on a pure relationship based on a divine connection rooted in love. Embracing relationship over legalism starts with knowing and seeking the heart of the Father.

When we approach others with a heart of empathy and compassion, we create space for genuine connections to flourish. Instead of judgment or condemnation, we choose to extend grace, understanding, and love. This is the position of the Heavenly Father in relating with His children. God is not looking for reasons to condemn us. When we view God as an unmerciful judge, we might inadvertently shy away from His presence, paralyzed by guilt and fear of condemnation. However, this fear contradicts the essence of God's nature. He does not seek to condemn but rather to embrace us profoundly, guiding us toward a life of righteousness and fulfillment. God's love and acceptance are not contingent upon our perfection but on our willingness to accept His grace and surrender our lives to His divine plan. When we understand His heart of love towards us, we will be free from the fear that emanates from guilt and condemnation (1 John 4:18; Romans 8:1).

Legalism often leads to a performance-driven mentality where we feel the need to meet specific standards to gain acceptance or approval. However, authentic connection is built upon mutual trust, honesty, and the freedom to be our authentic selves. The reason why many Christians feel far away from God is because of their pretense. They try to put their best foot forward before God, thinking that this will make them more acceptable before their Maker. The truth is that God sees everything that we are and that we are yet to do or become, yet He chose to love us. He is not surprised or embarrassed by our actions. When we allow God to see our vulnerabilities and imperfections, we give Him access to a deeper place in our hearts. God can only relate with the real you.

Embracing relationship over legalism also involves cultivating a spirit of forgiveness and grace. Don't be hard on yourself. Forgive yourself for any past mistakes. Many Christians still hold themselves hostage over what God had forgiven and let go of. Stop judging yourself. Rather than holding on to grudges or demanding perfection from one another, we should choose forgiveness. In doing so, we'll create an environment where relationships can thrive, where healing and reconciliation can occur, and where we can experience the transformative power of God.

True Connections with Others

Embracing relationship over legalism involves prioritizing love. Love is the foundation upon which genuine connection is built. A selfless, sacrificial love that seeks the well-being and flourishing of others. When we approach relationships with love as our guiding principle, we create a safe and nurturing space where individuals can be seen, valued, and embraced for who they truly are. Let us summon the courage to let go of legalistic tendencies and embrace the richness of a genuine relationship. May we cultivate empathy, forgiveness, and grace that fosters an environment where love can flourish. May our commitment to embracing relationship over legalism lead us to deeper connections, an authentic sense of belonging, and a greater sense of fulfillment and joy in our interactions with others.

Experiencing Freedom in Christ

As believers in Christ Jesus, we often find ourselves burdened by the weight of our mistakes, regrets, and the expectations placed upon us. We yearn for a sense of freedom—a liberation from the chains that hold us captive. In Christ, we discover a profound source of freedom that transcends our circumstances and liberates us from the bondage of sin, shame, and fear. It is an invitation to experience true freedom in every aspect of our lives.

Experiencing freedom in Christ begins with acknowledging our need for Him. We recognize that we are unable to free ourselves from the grip of sin and the consequences of our actions. In humility, we turn to Christ, who bore our sins on the cross and offers us forgiveness and redemption. It is through His sacrifice that we find liberation from the guilt and shame that weigh us down, experiencing the freedom to embrace a new identity as children of God.

In Christ, we are freed from the power of sin. Through His resurrection, He conquered sin and death, offering us victory and the power to overcome the patterns of sin that entangle us. He cut away our sinful nature by performing a spiritual circumcision in us (Colossians 2:11). As we surrender our lives to Him and rely on His strength, we find the freedom to resist temptation, break free from destructive habits, and live in alignment with God's purposes for us. The chains that once bound us are shattered. The sinful nature that gives access to the enemy to control us has been cut off, thus deactivating his power and control over us. Through Christ, we are set free to live a life of righteousness and holiness unto our God. Hallelujah!

Experiencing freedom in Christ also means letting go of our worries, anxieties, and fears. In a world filled with uncertainty and trials, we can find solace in Christ's assurance that He is with us always. We are invited to cast our burdens upon Him, knowing that He cares for us and has a perfect plan for our lives. This release allows us to experience a deep sense of peace and trust as we rest in the knowledge that we are held in the loving embrace of our Heavenly Father.

Furthermore, freedom in Christ involves embracing our true identity and worth. In Him, we are no longer defined by our past mistakes or the opinions of others. We are chosen, loved, and accepted as His beloved children. This newfound identity enables us to live confidently, free from the need to seek validation or approval from others. We can walk in the assurance that we are deeply loved and valued by our maker, and nothing can separate us from His love (Romans 8:38–39).

Experiencing freedom in Christ also means embracing the liberty to love and serve others selflessly. In Christ, we are called to love our neighbors as ourselves—to extend grace, compassion, and forgiveness to those around us. This freedom allows us to break free from the self-centeredness that hinders our relationships and to experience the joy of loving and serving others sacrificially without reservation. It is in giving of ourselves that we find true fulfillment and the freedom to live in accordance with God's command to love one another.

Pivotally, experiencing freedom in Christ is a lifelong journey. It requires a continual surrender of our lives to Him, a daily reliance on His grace, and a willingness to follow His leading. It is a journey of growing in our understanding of His love and the depths of His sacrifice for us. As we walk in this freedom, we discover the joy, peace, and purpose that come from living in an intimate relationship with our Savior.

May the freedom that is found in Christ be yours as you release the burdens of your past, your worries, and your fears. May you walk in the assurance of your identity and worth as His beloved child. May you love and serve others selflessly, experiencing the true fulfillment that comes from living in alignment with God's purposes. And may your journey of experiencing freedom in Christ be marked by joy, peace, and an ever-deepening intimacy with Him. Amen.

CHAPTER 8
ARE YOU THERE, GOD?

There are moments in our lives when we feel a disturbing sense of distance from God. We may wrestle with doubts, struggles, or the weight of our own shortcomings, making it seem as though God is far removed from us. We long for His presence, His guidance, and His comfort, but it feels as though we are wandering in a spiritual desert and disconnected from Him. In these seasons, prayers become a struggle, and we may even question if God still hears our prayers, if He still cares for us, or if He is even aware of our struggles. We may wonder why others seem to have a close and vibrant relationship with Him while we feel distant and alone. The ache within our hearts grows as we yearn to feel the nearness of God's embrace.

It is important to acknowledge that feeling isolated from God is not an unusual human experience. Even the most faithful and devout individuals have encountered moments of spiritual desolation at some point in their lives. The psalmist, in Psalm 13:1 (NKJV), cries out, "How long, O Lord? Will you forget me forever? How long will you hide your face from me?" This heartfelt plea resonates with our own cries when we feel distant from God. During such times, it is crucial to remember that our feelings do not always reflect the truth of God's presence. While our emotions may fluctuate and deceive us, the reality is that God's love and faithfulness remain constant. The prophet Isaiah assures us, "Can a mother forget the baby at her breast and have no compassion on the child she has borne? Though she may forget, I will not forget you!" (Isaiah 49:15, NIV). God's love for His children is unwavering, even when we feel disconnected.

Feeling disconnected from God can be an invitation to seek Him with renewed vigor and a deeper sense of vulnerability. It is an opportunity to examine our hearts, surrender our doubts and fears, and invite Him into the depths of our struggles. It is in these moments of raw honesty that we open ourselves to the transformative work of His love. Sometimes, feeling distant from God is an invitation for growth and refinement. It may be a season of testing where our faith is stretched and strengthened. Just as a tree's roots grow deeper during times of drought, our relationship with God can deepen as we press into Him, trusting that He is working in the midst of our perceived isolation. It could also mean that God is announcing the end of a certain season of our lives and preparing us for another level of His glory.

Those moments are not always easy. I remember vividly when God brought a particular season to an end in my life and how it transformed me forever. Night after night, for several months, I found myself drawn to my knees in prayer. My heart was heavy with burdens, and my soul longed for something more. The desire to pray consumed me, compelling me to seek solace and guidance in the presence of the Almighty. Although it was a very difficult time for me and my family, it became a catalyst for a new dimension of intimacy with the Holy Spirit for us. Initially, I was troubled by what I saw around me: the lack of accountability being displayed in unexpected quarters. I questioned why God would allow us to be in this type of situation when we were following His lead. I wondered why it seems as though the moral compass is missing in certain places. Where is the principle of fairness, honesty, and truth of the Word of God? How is it possible that individuals could so brazenly engage in some practices and do so without any sense of remorse and repentance? Such a thing would not have been permitted in society without raising a red flag! What troubled me even more was the deafening silence that ensued. It was as if everyone around had turned a blind eye to the situation. How is it that we claim to abide by the principles of righteousness and yet so readily engage in actions that contradict them?

Perhaps, I thought, there must have been a memo sent by God that I somehow missed. It seemed inconceivable that the world could have strayed so far from the path of virtue without some divine intervention. It was a stormy time in my Christian journey. My family felt abandoned by those we looked up to. I cried night after night as I poured out my heart to God. Tears mingling with my prayers. "God, we thought we were following your lead." My wife and I prayed ceaselessly, seeking answers. Then God assured us that it wasn't because of any wrongdoing on our part, but this has come so that His name would be glorified. We must journey on this path. It was a difficult time, yet a time of significant growth in our intimacy with the Lord.

This reminds me of the word of Peter in 1 Peter 2:19 (NLT), "For God is pleased when, conscious of his will, you patiently endure unjust treatment."

After months of waiting on God, I could sense a shift taking place within me. As I dug deeper, I also came to realize that the issue on the ground was not a matter of divine intervention but rather a crisis of conscience among humanity. God is still God. He has not shifted His stance on His standards for righteous living among His people. Unfairness, dishonesty, manipulations, and truth distortion have become the norm because we have allowed them to persist, not because God is no longer frowning on such. We have become complicit in our silence, choosing to turn a blind eye to the injustices we witness. We have ceased to hold ourselves and others accountable for our actions and theirs, allowing these vices to flourish unchecked. One may wonder: why are we so hesitant to speak out against these injustices? The answer lies in our fear—fear of retribution, fear of being ostracized, fear of standing alone. It is this fear that has shackled many and prevented us from reclaiming the moral high ground in the church and our society.

Within the walls of our church, there exists a troubling array of unsettling trends. It is disheartening to witness the glorification of immorality as if it were an admirable pursuit. However, we should be reminded of the words of the apostle Paul, who implored us to flee from sexual immorality, recognizing the harm it inflicts on our souls and relationships.

Furthermore, lies have become a prevalent skill set in today's ministry. We manipulate the truth to fit our narratives and manage situations and people for personal gain or to further our agenda. This practice directly contradicts the biblical command to speak the truth in love (Ephesians 4:15). It contradicts the teachings of the Bible, which explicitly warns against deceiving one another and emphasizes the significance of honesty and transparency. "Do not lie to each other, since you have taken off your old self with its practices" (Colossians 3:9, NIV). It erodes trust and credibility, making it difficult for others, especially the younger generation, to connect with the message we proclaim from the pulpit.

Instead of fostering an environment of unity and understanding, we allow offenses to spread rapidly, creating walls and divisions within our communities. As followers of God, we are called to embody truth and integrity, reflecting the very nature of a righteous and just God. However, in our relentless pursuit of success and influence, we have regrettably compromised our moral compass, leading to a disturbing misalignment between our words and our actions. Inevitably, this erosion of trust hinders our ability to effectively advance God's kingdom. It often feels as though, despite taking steps forward, our progress is relentlessly impeded by the opposing forces of the enemy seeking to undermine our efforts. It is undeniable that we face immense challenges within ourselves and our shared communities. It is crucial that we acknowledge these issues and strive to bring about positive change. Only by upholding values of virtue, honesty, and unity can we hope to overcome the obstacles that hinder our collective spiritual growth and continue to advance the kingdom of God.

The Need for a Genuine Repentance

To bring about a genuine revival and experience a true move of God in our generation, there must be a collective awakening to the need for repentance. We cannot continue to represent a God with whom we have no genuine relationship. We cannot expect to see a transformation in our nations, churches, and communities if we are not first transformed ourselves.

God is love. He loves His Children unconditionally, but we must humble ourselves and embrace His love. "Behold, God will not cast away the blameless, nor will He uphold the evildoers" (Job 8:20, NKJV). We must come to the throne of grace and repent. There must be a genuine repentance. What, then, does genuine repentance entail? It begins with acknowledging our failures and shortcomings, both individually and collectively. It involves turning away from the paths of deception and embracing the truth, even when it is painful or requires sacrifice. Genuine repentance calls for a change of heart and a change of behavior, aligning our lives with the teachings of Christ. Genuine repentance means dying to self, carrying our cross day by day, and following the footsteps of the master.

As the church, we need to set an example of repentance and humility. We must lead the way in renouncing the lies and deceit that have infiltrated our ranks. We need to foster a culture of accountability and transparency, where we encourage one another to live lives of integrity and truthfulness. Only through genuine repentance can we restore the credibility of our faith and effectively share the transformative power of God's love with our world. Once we embrace genuine repentance, a transformation will occur. Our priorities will shift, and our actions will align with our faith. We will be known for our integrity and authenticity, and the younger generation will see a tangible connection between what we preach and how we live. God's presence will no longer seem distant; instead, He will dwell among us, empowering us to carry out His kingdom work with boldness and effectiveness. God is always ready with an open hand when we repent and amend our ways.

Looking back now, God used those challenging moments to bring my family into a new season. He brought people into our lives who served as messengers of hope, reminding us of His promises and encouraging us to persevere. He provided opportunities for growth and learning, enabling us to develop new skills and perspectives that would be valuable in the coming season of our lives. He removed obstacles and opened doors, paving the way for new opportunities and blessings we could have never anticipated. Hallelujah!

As the psalmist declares, "The Lord is near to the brokenhearted and saves the crushed in spirit" (Psalm 34:18, ESV). It is important to surround ourselves with a community of believers who can offer support, encouragement, and perspective. Sharing our struggles with trusted friends or seeking counsel from spiritual mentors can provide the reassurance and guidance we need during times of spiritual distance.

Ultimately, feeling detached from God is a reminder that our faith journey is not always linear or predictable. It is a journey of hills and valleys, of mountaintop encounters and desert seasons. God, in His infinite wisdom, uses these times to refine us, to draw us closer to Him, and to deepen our reliance on His grace. As we navigate the complexities of feeling far away from God, may we find solace in the truth that His love knows no distance. Even when our emotions tell us otherwise, we can trust that He is near, patiently waiting for us to turn our hearts back to Him. In His presence, we find comfort, guidance, and the reassurance that He will never leave or forsake us (Hebrews 13:5).

CHAPTER 9
ADDRESSING THE DISTANCE
AND DISCONNECTION

When we feel remote and separated from God, it is critical that we address these feelings with honesty and vulnerability. We must fight the urge to withdraw even further or to wallow in misery and self-pity. Instead, we can take deliberate steps to close the gap and reestablish our connection with God.

First, we must examine our hearts and identify any impediments to our relationship with God. Is our conscience burdened by unresolved sins or unconfessed wrongdoings? Are we harboring unforgiveness in our hearts? Have we allowed distractions or worldly interests to take precedence over our pursuit of God in any aspect of our lives? Recognizing and repenting of these impediments can open the road to healing and restoration.

We can also look to the Scriptures for guidance, comfort, and truth in such times. The Word of God is alive and an active force that can bridge even the greatest chasms. As we read through its pages, we come across the experiences of people who have gone through seasons of isolation and estrangement from God. Their journeys serve as a reminder that we are not alone in our challenges and that God is steadfast in His promise to restore His children. Prayer becomes a vital lifeline in addressing the distance and disconnection we feel. In prayer, we pour out our hearts, share our doubts and fears, and express our longing for a renewed sense of closeness with God. Even if our prayers feel feeble or uncertain, we can trust that the Holy Spirit intercedes for us and carries our prayers to the Father's loving ear (Romans 8:26–27).

In times of disconnection, it might be helpful to seek the advice and support of trusted fellow Christians. Conversations with those who have traveled similar routes can provide new ideas, support, and a sense of camaraderie. We can draw on their wisdom and experience as we travel our own path back to God. As Paul said, whatever we are dealing with is common to man (1 Corinthians 10:13). Furthermore, participating in acts of worship and praise might help bridge the gap we feel. Even when our emotions are at odds with our desire to worship, we can choose to praise God, acknowledging His goodness, faithfulness, and sovereignty, reflecting on how He has brought us or others through difficult times in the past and resting in His faithfulness to do the same in our lives. Worship can be a tremendous trigger for us to enter His presence and align our hearts with His. It helps to shift our eyes from ourselves and fix them on the unchanging God with whom there is no shadow of turning (James 1:17).

We must cultivate patience and trust in God's timing. Reconnecting with God is not always an immediate process, and it may require perseverance on our part. We can rest assured that God is not distant by His own choosing but that His love continues to pursue us even in our seasons of feeling disconnected. As we surrender our hearts to Him and seek Him diligently, we can trust that He will draw near to us (James 4:8). Addressing the distance and disconnection we feel from God requires intentionality and an unwavering commitment to pursue Him. It is a journey of faith, where we choose to believe in His promises, trust in His love, and actively seek His presence. In this process, we may discover that our periods of distance have actually been opportunities for growth, refining our faith and deepening our dependence on Him.

As we embark on the journey of addressing the distance and disconnection, may we do so with a sense of hope, knowing that God is always ready to restore and reconcile His children to Himself. May we surrender our doubts and fears to Him, trusting that He is faithful to bridge the gap and fill our hearts with a renewed sense of His love, grace, and nearness.

Unforgiveness: A Formidable Barrier

Unforgiveness could erect a formidable barrier, a wall of separation between God and man. That is why it is important that I mention it in this book. When someone wrongs us, whether intentionally or unintentionally, our natural inclination may be to hold onto the pain, resentment, and anger; however, this not only harms us emotionally and mentally, but it also hinders our connection with God. The Bible teaches us to be kind and tenderhearted, to forgive one another, just as God forgave us through Jesus Christ (Ephesians 4:32). These words emphasize the importance of forgiveness in our spiritual journey. God, being the embodiment of love and mercy, sent His son Jesus to redeem humanity from their sins. Through Christ's sacrifice, we were granted forgiveness for our transgressions. This act of forgiveness is a fundamental value in Christianity, and it should also govern our relationships with others.

Many people talk, teach, and preach more about forgiveness but care less about walking in total forgiveness. We hear more about forgiveness on the pulpit but see less of the manifestation among us. When we hold onto unforgiveness, we not only create a barrier between ourselves and the person who wronged us, but we also create a barrier between ourselves and God. By harboring bitterness, resentment, and an unwillingness to forgive, we distance ourselves from the love, grace, and peace that God wants to pour into our lives.

In Matthew 6:14, Jesus said that our receiving forgiveness from God is contingent upon our forgiveness for others. This is serious! Unforgiveness can consume our hearts, cloud our judgment, and hinder our spiritual growth. It prevents us from truly experiencing the transformative power of God's forgiveness in our own lives. We fall short of God's perfection because we are imperfect beings. However, through our repentance and seeking of forgiveness, we can experience a deep connection and restoration with God. By refusing to extend that same forgiveness to others, we limit our own ability to receive forgiveness and spiritual growth. Unforgiveness creates a cycle of hurt, resentment, and conflict, preventing genuine healing and reconciliation. By letting go of unforgiveness, we open ourselves up to healing, reconciliation, and the possibility of restoring broken relationships.

Someone once asked me how I knew I had fully forgiven someone. I said that when you place everything in the hands of God, when you entrust all matters to God, believing that He will handle everything according to His perfect will, that means you let Him decide the outcome. Even if God chooses to forgo the punishment of the wrongdoer, you still have faith in God's decision. That is how you know that you have truly forgiven. Overcoming unforgiveness requires personal introspection, humility, and a willingness to let go of past hurts. It involves a conscious choice to release the pain, anger, and resentment, recognizing that holding onto them only serves to distance us from God and obstruct our spiritual growth. When we make the decision to forgive, we align ourselves with God's character and His pursuit of peace. We realize that what we gain by staying in alignment with God is far greater than any satisfaction we may derive from avenging ourselves or holding grudges against our offenders. We can only fully understand and feel God's love and restoration through forgiveness. For if you forgive other people their sins when they sin against you, your Heavenly Father will also forgive you, Jesus Himself stated. However, if you don't pardon the crimes of others, your Father won't pardon yours (Matthew 6:14–15). We must also extend the same forgiveness—to ourselves. Holding onto guilt, past mistakes, shame, or resentment only further hinders our ability to reconnect with God. Through the power of His love, we release the burdens of the past, choosing to forgive ourselves. In doing so, we open the door for God's healing touch.

Seeking Reconciliation and Restoration

When we find ourselves in a place of distance and disconnection from God, we are called to actively seek reconciliation and restoration. It is a path that calls for bravery, honesty, and a willingness to let God's love work on our hearts. We find that God is waiting for us at the end of this road, with open arms, to welcome us back and repair our connection with Him. Seeking reconciliation and restoration begins with a humble acknowledgment of our own needs. We recognize our longing for God's presence and the ways in which we may have contributed to the distance we feel. With open hearts, we humbly approach the Father, confessing our doubts, our sins, and our shortcomings. We lay them at His feet, trusting in His mercy and grace to bring healing and restoration.

As we seek restoration, we must actively engage with God's Word. The Scriptures serve as a compass, guiding us toward truth and providing wisdom for our journey. In reading and meditating on the Word, we open ourselves to God's voice and allow His truth to shape our thoughts, actions, and perceptions. His Word becomes a lamp to our feet and a light to our path, leading us back into His loving embrace. Prayer becomes an integral part of our pursuit of reconciliation and restoration. We pour out our hearts to God, expressing our longings, doubts, and hopes. We seek His guidance, His wisdom, and His presence. In prayer, we commune with the Father, entrusting our lives to His care and inviting Him to work in and through us. We open ourselves to His transforming power and surrender to His perfect timing, knowing that He makes all things beautiful in its time (Ecclesiastes 3:11).

In seeking reconciliation and restoration, we discover that God's love knows no bounds. He eagerly awaits our return, ready to receive us with open arms. As we surrender our hearts to Him, He extends forgiveness, healing, and a renewed sense of purpose. Our relationship with Him is mended, and we find ourselves embraced by the Father's love, once again walking in close communion with Him.

May our journey of seeking reconciliation and restoration be marked by faith, humility, and a deep desire to be reconciled with the One who loves us unconditionally. May we open our hearts to His transforming power and experience the fullness of His grace. And may our lives be a testament to the redemptive work of God, drawing others into His embrace of reconciliation and restoration.

CHAPTER 10

THE FATHER OF SPIRIT

As we embark on this glorious journey into the depths of God's essence, we are captivated by a resplendent revelation of His majestic being. He, indeed, is the magnificent Father of spirits, as the Scriptures in Hebrews 12:9 declare. Let this revelation resonate within the depths of your soul, for it unveils the profound truth that we are not mere mortal beings confined to this earthly realm. Rather, we are magnificent spiritual beings, intricately fashioned in the very likeness of our Heavenly Father, the Creator of all things. Hallelujah!

The Almighty, who is the Father of spirits, possesses an intimate knowledge of the very depths of our souls, our deepest longings, and our fervent yearnings. He beholds with insight, penetrating the very depths of our being, where our authentic essence abides. He possesses an intimate knowledge of our thoughts, our emotions, and the deepest desires that reside within the depths of our being. Just as an earthly father understands and cherishes his precious children, so does our Heavenly Father, in all His glory and majesty. He truly comprehends and passionately loves us, His beloved children, as magnificent spiritual beings. "I will be a true Father to you, and you will be my beloved sons and daughters" (2 Corinthians 6:18, TPT), says the Lord Yahweh Almighty.

This heavenly revelation fills our hearts with an overwhelming sense of peace. We are not mere wanderers on this earthly path; we have a Heavenly Father who possesses intimate knowledge and a fervent concern for our spiritual and physical welfare. He graciously leads us, divinely shields us, and tenderly nourishes our souls as a compassionate earthly father does for his beloved offspring. He ardently desires for us to thrive and blossom in our spiritual journeys and to prosper as His cherished offspring. Oh, beloved child of the Most High, hear the melodious whispers of the Heavenly Father, who beckons us to embark on a journey of profound fellowship with His glorious presence! He yearns for our spirits to intertwine with His Spirit so that we may encounter the life-altering might of His glorious presence. By the anointing of the Holy Spirit, the Almighty God graciously takes up residence within the depths of our being, imparting wisdom, leading us in the paths of righteousness, and endowing us with supernatural strength to fulfill our heavenly calling (John 14:16–17).

Our spirits find rest and fulfillment in the embrace of our Heavenly Father. It is in His presence that we find solace from the weariness of life, the burdens of the world, and the struggles of our spirits. Just as a child seeks the comforting embrace of a loving father, we can seek refuge in the loving arms of our Heavenly Father, knowing that His love and care for our spirits are unwavering. As the Father of spirits, God invites us into a deep and personal relationship with Him. He calls us His children and offers us the privilege of calling Him "Abba, Father" (Romans 8:15, NIV). This intimate term of endearment captures the tenderness and closeness of our connection with Him. It reflects the Father's heart, which beats with love and compassion for His children.

Nurturing Our Spirit

In a beautiful connection with the Father of spirits, we witness His glorious and life-changing action deep within us. The Almighty miraculously shapes our minds into the flawless image of His loving Son, the Anointed one, Jesus Christ (Romans 8:29). He instills love, joy, peace, patience, kindness, goodness, faithfulness, gentleness, and self-control (Galatians 5:22–23). He cleanses and sanctifies our spirits so we can mirror His character. Understanding God as the Father of spirits also instills duty. We must honor and cherish our spirits. We must invest in the thing that grows our spiritual life. Prayer, meditation on His Word, worship, and spiritual disciplines grow our spirits. We yield to His will and follow His counsel. The Father of spirits teaches us that spiritual well-being is crucial. Our spirits are eternal and will live with our Heavenly Father forever. May we seek His presence, hear His voice, and let His Spirit lead and guide us. May our lives reflect the beauty and grace of being children of the Father of spirits, shining His light into a world in need of His love.

Learning from Earthly Fathers' Discipline

As we reflect on the role of fathers in our lives, we can confidently recognize that they play a significant part in shaping our character, values, and understanding of discipline. Earthly fathers, imperfect as they may be, offer valuable and assured lessons in discipline that we can apply to our spiritual journey. Discipline from our earthly fathers is rooted in unwavering love. Just as a loving father desires the absolute best for his children, God, our Heavenly Father, disciplines us out of His deep and absolute love for us. Earthly fathers correct and guide us when we go astray. They teach us the importance of making wise choices and instill in us a sense of responsibility. They set boundaries and enforce rules, not to restrict us but to protect and guide us toward a flourishing life.

When an earthly father disciplines, he does so with a clear and long-term vision in mind. He seeks to shape his children's character, equipping them with the tools they need to navigate the complexities of life. Similarly, God's discipline is purposeful and assured, aiming to refine our character and draw us closer to Him. He uses discipline as a means to mold us into the image of His Son, Jesus Christ, so that we may bear the fruit of righteousness (Hebrews 12:11).

Discipline from an earthly father teaches us about choices and consequences. When we disobey or make poor choices, we experience the natural consequences of our actions. This understanding of cause and effect cultivates a sense of responsibility and helps us to develop discernment. Likewise, God's discipline reminds us that our actions carry consequences. He allows us to face the repercussions of our decisions, not to punish us but to help us learn and grow in wisdom.

In the midst of discipline, earthly fathers display a balance of firmness and compassion. They provide correction and guidance with an understanding heart, recognizing their children's humanity and inherent worth. Similarly, God's discipline is marked by His absolute, compassionate nature. He corrects us with absolute gentleness and love, always mindful of our fragility. He desires our growth and restoration, even in the midst of discipline. Earthly fathers also demonstrate the importance of forgiveness and restoration. When we repent and seek reconciliation after a transgression, a loving father extends forgiveness, welcoming us back into his embrace. In the same way, our Heavenly Father offers absolute forgiveness and restoration when we turn to Him in repentance. He is always ready to receive us, to heal our wounds, and to restore our relationship with Him.

Learning from earthly fathers' discipline can also teach us about perseverance and endurance. Earthly fathers often discipline with the intention of helping their children build resilience and overcome challenges. They encourage grit in the face of adversity, teaching us not to give up but to press on. Likewise, God's discipline strengthens our faith and perseverance. It develops within us the ability to endure trials, knowing with assurance that He is working all things together for our good (Romans 5:3–5; 8:28). As we reflect on the lessons we learn from earthly fathers' discipline, we can confidently recognize that their imperfect yet valuable guidance can help shape our understanding of discipline from our Heavenly Father. Through their actions, they provide glimpses of God's unwavering love, His purposeful discipline, His compassion, and His absolute desire for our growth and restoration.

May we honor and appreciate the earthly fathers in our lives for the lessons they have taught us. And as we grow in our understanding of God's discipline, may we embrace His correction and guidance with humility and gratitude, knowing with absolute certainty that His discipline stems from His deep and absolute love for us. May we allow His discipline to shape us, refine our character, and draw us into a closer relationship with Him.

Willingly Submitting to the Father for Spiritual Growth

In our journey of spiritual growth, willingly submitting to the Father becomes a transformative act of surrender and trust. It is an acknowledgment that we are not the masters of our lives but rather beloved children under the guidance and care of our Heavenly Father. Through this voluntary act of submission, we open ourselves to His loving discipline, His transformative work, and His abundant grace. Submitting to the Father requires humility—an understanding that we do not have all the answers and that our wisdom is limited. It is an admission that our ways may not align with His perfect plan. Just as a child relies on the wisdom and guidance of their earthly father, we recognize that our Heavenly Father knows what is best for us. He sees the bigger picture, understands the intricacies of our lives, and desires to lead us on the path of righteousness.

In willingly submitting to the Father, we demonstrate trust—an unwavering belief in His goodness, faithfulness, and love for us. We trust that His plans for our lives surpass our own, and we surrender our desires and ambitions to His divine wisdom. Like a child who places complete trust in their father's guidance, we entrust ourselves to the care of our Heavenly Father, confident that He will lead us along the paths of righteousness for His name's sake (Psalm 23:3). Submitting to the Father is an act of surrender—a letting go of our own will and embracing His will for our lives. It is a recognition that our selfish desires and ambitions can hinder our spiritual growth. By surrendering our desires, dreams, and plans to Him, we make room for His purposes to unfold. We align our hearts with His, inviting Him to shape and mold us according to His perfect design.

In this act of submission, we find freedom. We are liberated from the burden of trying to control our own lives, for we trust that our Heavenly Father holds us in His capable hands. We release the need to conform to the pressures and expectations of the world, knowing that our identity and worth are found in Him alone. We experience the joy and peace that come from living in alignment with His will. Willingly submitting to the Father also opens us to His transformative work within us. As we surrender, He molds our hearts, purifies our motives, and refines our character. Through His Spirit, He empowers us to overcome our weaknesses and align our lives with His truth. It is in this surrender that we experience true spiritual growth—a growth that shapes us into the likeness of His Son, Jesus Christ.

In our journey of willingly submitting to the Father, we are not alone. We are empowered by His grace, which sustains us and enables us to persevere. We are guided by His Spirit, who empowers us to walk in obedience and surrender. And we are supported by a community of fellow believers who walk alongside us, encouraging and challenging us to continually surrender to God's will. As we willingly submit to the Father for our spiritual growth, we recognize that this is an ongoing process—an invitation to continually surrender and align ourselves with His will. It requires daily surrender, a posture of openness, and a willingness to let go of our own desires and preferences. But in this act of submission, we find abundant grace, transformative growth, and a deepening relationship with our Heavenly Father.

It pays to willingly submit to the Father, knowing that He has our best interests at heart. May we trust in His wisdom, surrender our will to His, and experience the fullness of His love and grace. And may our surrender lead us to a life of deep spiritual growth, where we reflect His character and bring glory to His name.

CHAPTER 11
GROWING SPIRITUALLY

God did not call us to a life of complacency and stagnancy. We are commanded to live fruitful and thriving lives as followers of Christ. God wants His followers to develop spiritually and accept the role He has for them. Realizing that our walk with God is a process that is constantly advancing is crucial. It is easy in today's fast-paced environment to become complacent and spiritually dormant. Our connection with God can easily fall to the wayside if we let ourselves become consumed by the demands of daily life. However, God has called us to do so much more than just go through the motions of life.

Just as a stagnant pond lacks liveliness and vitality, a stagnant believer lacks the vibrancy and passion that God desires for us. In contrast, a life of growth and purpose is marked by a deep sense of joy, peace, and fulfillment. God's will for us is to be dynamic, not fixed. He wants to lead us in an experience of personal development and growth. A life full of unending adventures. Just as a caterpillar goes through stages of metamorphosis before becoming a beautiful butterfly, we go through spiritual metamorphosis in order to reach our full potential in Christ. We come to the cross as we are, but we are never to remain as we came. Salvation is only a doorway to the supernatural and dynamic life that God has prepared for us. In order to go on, we must let go of the past and take hold of the future God has in store for us.

Dealing with Stagnancy

Growth leads to fulfillment. This is one of the reasons why God has not called us into a life of stagnancy. When we are actively growing in our faith and seeking God's will for our lives, we experience a sense of purpose and fulfillment that cannot be found elsewhere. It is through this growth that we are able to discover our true identity and live out the destiny that God has planned for us. God has equipped us with everything we need to grow and thrive in our relationship with Him. He has given us His Word, the Bible, as a guide for our lives. It is through studying and meditating on His Word that we gain wisdom and understanding. God has also given us His Holy Spirit to empower and guide us in our journey of growth. The Holy Spirit convicts us of sin, leads us into truth, and enables us to live according to God's will.

In order to avoid stagnancy in our Christian journey, it is important for us to be intentional about our spiritual growth. This means setting aside time each day to spend in prayer and Bible study. It means actively seeking opportunities to serve and make a difference in the lives of others. It means surrounding ourselves with like-minded believers who can encourage and challenge us in our walk with God. It is also important for us to be willing to step out of our comfort zones and take risks for God. Growth requires stepping into the unknown and trusting that God will guide us every step of the way. We must be open to new experiences and be willing to embrace the challenges and opportunities that God brings our way.

As believers, let us embrace the call to a life of growth and avoid the trap of stagnancy. Let us commit ourselves to seeking God's will and following His leading in every area of our lives. May we continually strive to grow in our faith and fulfill the destiny that God has prepared for us. Remember, God has not called us into a life of dormancy but one of purpose, growth, and abundant life.

Signs of Stagnancy in Spiritual Growth

Stagnancy in spiritual growth can manifest in various ways. It may be characterized by a lack of enthusiasm or passion for the spiritual path, a feeling of being disconnected or lost, or a sense of being stuck in old patterns and habits. It can be a lack of new experiences with God, loss of the joy of salvation, lack of desire, or hunger for the things of God. Other signs of stagnancy include resistance to change and a tendency to rely on external sources for validation and guidance.

As a stagnant pond dries up in the heat of the sun, such a believer's life cannot withstand the heat brought by the pressures of life. This is not the desire of the Father for us. He wants us to stay plugged into His ever-increasing grace. To have a deeper and ever-increasing knowledge of Him and to be a conduit through which His will is established on the earth on a daily basis.

The danger in stagnancy is that sometimes someone may be stagnant and not be aware of it. It is possible to be active and busy doing God's work and still be stagnant. We begin to ride on the euphoria of people's applause and accolades and ignore the gentle pull of the Holy Spirit on us to come away to be with

Him so He can equip us for more. We become engrossed with what men see as great work for God and forget that there is no arrival point in our Christian journey here on earth. There is greater work to be done for Him. There is more capacity available to those who hunger and thirst for more of Him. There is no room for hibernation.

If you notice any of these signs in your own spiritual journey, it is important to take them as an opportunity for reflection and growth. Stagnancy is not a permanent state; it is simply an indication that there is room for growth and transformation.

Overcoming Obstacles to Spiritual Growth

Obstacles are a natural part of the spiritual journey. They come in various forms, such as self-doubt, fear, attachment, and distractions. However, it is through overcoming these obstacles that we experience the most profound growth and transformation.

One way to overcome obstacles is through self-reflection and introspection. By examining our thoughts, emotions, and beliefs, we can acquire a deeper understanding of ourselves and the obstacles holding us back. This self-awareness allows us to make conscious choices and take deliberate actions toward our spiritual growth. *In intimacy, He shows you obstacles and empowers you to overcome them.*

Spiritual Dependency

Proverbs 3:5 (ESV) exhorts us to "Trust in the Lord with all your heart, and do not lean on your own understanding."

Our relationship with Christ is what the Gospel is all about. We have been freed from our slavery to sin and joined with Him in His death. Dependency is necessary for this union. We can only be made righteous and produce the fruits of righteousness in Him. Paul declares, "I have been crucified with Christ" (Galatians 2:20, ESV), and he means this. "Christ now lives in me; it is no longer I who is alive" (Galatians 2:20, ESV). According to Galatians 2:20 (ESV), "And the life I now live in the flesh I live by faith in the Son of God, who loved me and gave himself for me." Just like branches will never outgrow a tree, we will never outgrow the vine. Jesus said in John 15:5 (NIV), "I am the vine; you are the branches. If you remain in me and I in you, you will bear much fruit; apart from me, you can do nothing."

God's original plan does not include any provision for His creation, including humanity, to be self-sufficient. God is all-sufficient by Himself. He is fully dependent upon everything else in creation (Colossians 1:17). We would be totally destroyed if the Lord ever ceased "intervening" in our lives, even for a split second! For those who are in Christ, we continually become more aware of how totally dependent we are on Him, and the only way we can completely experience life in Him is by giving ourselves over to Him.

Seeking Guidance from Spiritual Mentors or Leaders

Seeking guidance from spiritual mentors or leaders can greatly enhance our spiritual growth. These individuals have a wealth of wisdom and experience that they can share with us, providing us with guidance, support, and inspiration on our journey.

A spiritual mentor or leader can help us navigate the challenges and uncertainties of the spiritual path. They can provide perspectives and insights that we may not have considered on our own. They can also provide us with practical tools and techniques to deepen our spiritual practice and overcome obstacles.

When seeking spiritual mentorship or leadership, it is critical to engage with an open mind and heart. It is also important to find someone who resonates with your own biblical beliefs and values, as this will create a strong foundation for growth and learning.

CHAPTER 12

THE PLACE OF SPIRITUAL HUNGER

Spiritual hunger is a significant tool for spiritual growth, and it holds the power to transform our lives in profound ways. In the pursuit of a meaningful and fulfilling life, there exists an inherent longing within each one of us. It is a desire that transcends the physical and material, reaching the depths of our souls. This profound yearning is commonly referred to as "spiritual hunger." It is an inner craving for righteousness, a quest for a deeper connection with something greater than ourselves.

In the Gospel of Matthew 5:6 (NKJV), the Bible states, "Blessed are those who hunger and thirst for righteousness, for they shall be filled." This verse encapsulates the belief that the pursuit of spiritual nourishment is not only virtuous but also leads to satisfaction and fulfillment. It emphasizes the importance of longing for righteousness as an essential step toward attaining a higher spiritual status. It is essential to distinguish between genuine spiritual hunger and the pursuit of spiritual experiences solely for personal gain or validation. True spiritual hunger is rooted in authenticity and sincerity; it is driven by a genuine desire to align with God in His divine plan for our lives. It involves a willingness to confront oneself, transcend ego-driven desires, and embrace personal growth with humility and grace.

In a world that often emphasizes material achievements and external validation, nurturing our spiritual hunger can be a transformative and life-affirming endeavor. It provides us with the tools to navigate the ups and downs of life and find meaning in adversity. Spiritual hunger is not a destination but rather an ongoing journey of self-discovery and development. It is what drives our pursuit of God and keeps the fire burning within us. It requires dedication, patience, sacrifice, and an open heart.

King David was a man driven by an unrelenting hunger for God. In Psalm 42, verse 1, he described his desire for God as the desperation of a deer panting after water. In chapter 63, he mentioned how his soul longs for God. He was indeed a man after God's heart! An insatiable hunger for the things of God is essential to experiencing the deeper depths of God. For as we hunger and thirst for the things of God, we are offered an inexhaustible feast of wisdom and access to the deeper thing that God had prepared for those who diligently seek Him.

What Is Spiritual Hunger?

Spiritual hunger is not to be confused with physical hunger or the desire for material possessions. While these desires are valid in their own rights, spiritual hunger refers to a different kind of craving. It is an ache within the depths of our being that prompts us to seek after God, to find solace and meaning beyond the material realm. It is a yearning for more of God, more of the presence and power of the Holy Spirit. Recognizing and acknowledging our spiritual hunger is the first step towards nurturing the spirit of man within. It requires a willingness to explore our innermost selves and let go of ourselves in order to have more of God. This introspection allows us to identify the areas of our lives that lack spiritual fulfillment and release such areas to God to begin the transformative process. By acknowledging our hunger, we open ourselves up to growth and self-improvement that goes beyond the physical realm, setting the stage for a meaningful and fulfilling spiritual journey. "As the deer pants for the water brooks, So pants my soul for You, O God" (Psalm 42:1, NKJV).

It is worth noting that nurturing our spiritual hunger is not a one-time endeavor. Just as our physical bodies require nourishment throughout our lives, our spiritual selves also demand continuous attention and care. By committing to regular spiritual practices and seeking out new experiences with the Holy Spirit, we can sustain continuous spiritual growth that fills the void within our souls.

In the hustle and bustle of our daily lives, it is easy to overlook the depth of our spiritual hunger. Yet, tending to this inner longing is essential if we are to live purposeful and fulfilled lives. By recognizing and embracing the longing of the spirit within, we embark on a transformative journey towards self-discovery and a deeper connection with the Spirit of God as we chase after Him with our whole being.

Spiritual hunger leads us to seek the Lord daily. "You will seek me and find me when you seek me with all your heart" (Jeremiah 29:13, NIV).

The Importance of Spiritual Hunger

The importance of spiritual hunger lies in its ability to awaken our greatest potential because it is in a deep connection with God that we can become the best version of what we were created to be. Spiritual hunger acts as a driving force that pushes us beyond complacency and mediocrity, encouraging us to seek personal transformation and self-realization until we become like Christ. It compels us to question reality and our role in it, leading to a greater sense of purpose and fulfillment. As physical hunger is a sign of health, spiritual hunger depicts spiritual vitality that a Christian is alive.

When we embrace our spiritual hunger, we embark on a profound journey of self-discovery and expansion. It opens us up to the treasures of heaven. As the hunger for personal spiritual growth intensifies, so does the desire to share the fruits of that growth with the world. It inspires acts of kindness, compassion, and love.

Cultivating a Hunger for God's Presence

As human beings, we are wired for connection—with others and with something greater than ourselves. Deep within our souls, there is a longing to experience the presence of God, to encounter His love, and to be transformed by His power. Cultivating a hunger for God's presence is a journey of the heart, a pursuit of intimacy that draws us closer to the very essence of our Creator. To cultivate a hunger for God's presence, we must first acknowledge the depth of our need. We recognize that our hearts are restless until they find their rest in Him, as St. Augustine beautifully articulated.

It is an admission that the pursuits of this world, no matter how enticing, can never fully satisfy the hunger within us. We yearn for something greater, something transcendent—God Himself.

The journey of cultivating a hunger for God's presence begins with intentional seeking. We set aside time and create space in our lives to seek His face, to listen for His voice, and to be still in His presence. This seeking God involves prayer as we open ourselves to encounter God in the midst of our daily lives. As we seek, we also engage with God's Word—the Bible. The Scriptures are not mere words on a page but a living, breathing revelation of God's character and His desires for us. By immersing ourselves in His Word, we are drawn deeper into His presence and nourished by His truth. The Bible becomes a roadmap that guides our hunger, leading us to a more profound understanding of who God is and igniting a greater desire to experience His presence.

To cultivate a hunger for God's presence, we must be willing to surrender and let go of the distractions and attachments that hinder our pursuit. We relinquish control and allow God to take His rightful place at the center of our lives. This surrender involves releasing the idols and false dependencies that vie for our attention and affection, creating space for God to fill the void within us with His love and grace. A hunger for God's presence is nourished by engaging in acts of worship and adoration. Through praise, we express our reverence and gratitude for who God is and what He has done. In worship, whether through music, art, or other forms of creative expression, we open our hearts to the beauty and majesty of God's touch. In these moments, we are transported into the very presence of God, where our hunger is satisfied, and our souls find rest.

Furthermore, cultivating a hunger for God's presence involves embracing a posture of humility and dependency. We recognize that we are creatures in need of our Creator, and we humbly approach Him with reverence and awe. In our dependence, we acknowledge that apart from Him, we can do nothing, and it is through Him that we find true fulfillment and purpose. Community plays a vital role in cultivating a hunger for God's presence. We gather with fellow believers to worship, to pray, and to encourage one another in our faith journeys. In the company of like-minded individuals, our hunger for God's presence is nurtured and strengthened. We inspire and challenge one another, sharing testimonies of God's faithfulness and spurring each other on in pursuing His presence.

Ultimately, cultivating a hunger for God's presence is a lifelong journey. It requires a daily commitment to seek Him, to surrender, and to nurture our relationship with Him. It is not a one-time event but a continuous process of transformation and growth. As we cultivate this hunger, we discover that God meets us in the depths of our longing, filling us with His presence, love, and joy.

Embracing God's Promises for Joy and Growth

As human beings, we have a deep desire for joy and growth in our lives. We long for a sense of purpose, fulfillment, and peace. In the midst of life's challenges and uncertainties, God offers us His promises—assurances that He is with us, that He cares for us, and that He has plans for our well-being. Embracing these promises opens the door to a journey of joy and growth rooted in our relationship with Him. One of God's promises is the gift of joy. He assures us that true joy is found in Him alone, independent of our circumstances. It is a joy that transcends fleeting happiness and is grounded in the unchanging nature of His love and presence. As we embrace this promise, we discover that joy is not dependent on external factors but is cultivated through a deepening relationship with our Heavenly Father. In His presence, we find a wellspring of joy that sustains us through the highs and lows of life.

God also promises growth and transformation. He invites us into a journey of becoming more like Him, of being conformed to the image of His Son, Jesus Christ. This growth occurs as we surrender to His leading, allowing His Spirit to work within us, shaping our character, and guiding our choices. Embracing this promise means embracing the process of growth, even when it feels challenging or uncomfortable. It involves trusting that God is at work in us, molding us into vessels that reflect His love, grace, and truth. To embrace God's promises for joy and growth, we must cultivate a posture of trust and surrender. It is a conscious choice to release our grip on control and place our trust in the One who holds our lives in His hands. This surrender allows God to work in us, to bring about the transformation and growth that He desires for us. As we let go and surrender our plans, dreams, and fears to Him, we discover the freedom and peace that come from resting in His faithfulness.

Embracing God's promises also involves cultivating a mindset of gratitude and thanksgiving. Gratitude shifts our focus from what is lacking to what we have been given. It reminds us of God's goodness, provision, and faithfulness in our lives. As we cultivate a heart of gratitude, we open ourselves to receive the abundant blessings that God pours out upon us, deepening our joy and fostering a spirit of contentment.

Dear believer, embrace the invitation to cultivate a hunger for God's presence, allowing our souls to be captivated by His beauty and grace. May we seek Him with all our hearts, knowing that as we draw near to Him, He draws near to us. And may our hunger for God's presence become a consuming fire, guiding us into a deeper intimacy with the One who satisfies our every longing.

Prayer: A Tool for Spiritual Growth

"As he was praying, the appearance of his face changed, and his clothes became as bright as a flash of lightning" (Luke 9:29, NIV). These words, found in the New Testament of the Bible, depict a profound transformation that occurred during a moment of intimate connection with God. This passage holds a deeper significance of the transforming power of prayer in the life of a believer.

Prayer is more than asking and receiving from God. Prayer has the power to transform our lives. It is a transformative tool, enabling personal growth and inner transformation. It acts as a conduit for God's power, nurturing our spiritual growth and connecting us with the realms of God's glory. In prayer, we tap into the divine source of love, wisdom, and healing, bringing about a positive shift in our thoughts, emotions, and behaviors.

It empowers us to break free from negative patterns, release emotional baggage, and cultivate a mindset of positivity and resilience.

The change in appearance of Jesus, as described in Luke 9:29, suggests a transcendence of the physical realm and a glimpse into the realms of the Spirit. This transformation goes beyond mere superficial changes in one's countenance; it signifies a profound internal shift. When we engage in prayer, we open ourselves up to the possibility of experiencing a deep spiritual connection, which can result in personal growth. This was evident in the lives of the apostles. In Acts chapter 2, the apostles received the baptism of the Holy Spirit. We see another instance in Acts 4:31 (AMP), "When they had prayed, the place where they were meeting together was shaken [a sign of God's presence]; and they were all filled with the Holy Spirit and began to speak the word of God with boldness and courage." Something had happened to them. They were being changed from the inside out to the extent that the same set of people who were afraid when their master was arrested were now filled with boldness and courage to preach the Gospel. Their growth continued such that the events recorded in Acts 5 demonstrate a new dimension of the power of God through the apostles. In verse 15 of Acts chapter 5 (NIV), "As a result, people brought the sick into the streets and laid them on beds and mats so that at least Peter's shadow might fall on some of them as he passed by." These men have grown so much in their walk with God that the shadow of Peter could heal, and the *handkerchiefs and aprons* of Paul could cast out the devil (Acts 19:12).

Rediscovering the Beauty
and Significance of Spiritual Things

There are moments in our spiritual journey when we long to rediscover the beauty and significance of spiritual things. This longing invites us to embark on a journey of reawakening and renewal. Rediscovering spiritual beauty starts with a shift in perspective. We open our hearts and minds to the wonders around us—the intricate details of creation, the blessings we receive, and moments of divine intervention. Cultivating awe and gratitude allows us to see God's hand at work, reigniting our wonder and appreciation. Nurturing our relationship with God is vital in this process. Just as a neglected friendship requires intentional effort to restore, our connection with our Heavenly Father thrives when we invest time and energy.

Approaching spiritual matters with childlike curiosity and humility is crucial. Like children exploring the world with wonder, we seek fresh perspectives, eager to learn and grow. We ask questions, seek understanding, and embrace new revelations, knowing that God reveals Himself to those with childlike faith. Embracing mystery is also part of reconnecting with spiritual significance. Our faith rests on divine mysteries beyond human comprehension. Accepting this invites us to trust in God's love and wisdom, finding joy in the journey of discovery. Worship services, acts of service, and moments of silence deepen our awareness of God's presence and work. These practices connect us, renew us, and cultivate a vibrant faith. Drawing inspiration from saints and spiritual giants fuels our rediscovery. Their testimonies and examples point us toward the profound beauty of a life rooted in

God. Learning from them ignites a desire to seek the same depth of relationship and intimacy. Intentional gratitude is essential in rediscovering spiritual beauty. Cultivating a grateful heart helps us recognize countless blessings, big and small. Expressing gratitude to God opens us to a deeper appreciation of the spiritual dimensions of life. It fuels our desire to seek God, abide in His presence, and live with awe and reverence.

As we embark on this journey of rediscovery, let your heart anticipate with openness. May we seek God wholeheartedly, knowing He reveals Himself to those who seek Him. May gratitude fill our hearts as we appreciate His creation and blessings. May our spirits be stirred with renewed awe and wonder as we encounter the depths of His love and the beauty of a life lived in communion with Him.

CHAPTER 13
THE MYSTERY OF GOD'S PRESENCE

When we come to God through our Lord Jesus Christ, the first thing we encounter is the Father's embrace. We come to the realization that the Father had been waiting all along for us to come back to His loving arms. Then, the Holy Spirit begins to work in us, bringing the awareness of God's love and presence into our lives.

When the prodigal son returned to his father, the father asked that he be clothed with a robe. The robe is not merely a garment but carries a deeper meaning. It represents the glory the father confers upon his son. In biblical texts, glory often denotes God's divine presence and favor. Through the gift of the robe, the father reveals the magnitude of his joy at his son's return and signifies the restoration of his son's spiritual connection with the Father. It is a visual representation of the prodigal son's redemption, a fresh start, and a reinstatement into grace.

To understand the significance of the robe in the prodigal son's homecoming, we must first reflect on the origin of humankind's separation from God. In the Garden of Eden, Adam and Eve's disobedience resulted in their sudden awareness of their nakedness. Their glory covering was removed because of their disobedience; this pivotal moment symbolized their fall from grace and departure from God's intended glory. "For all have sinned and come short of the glory of God" (Romans 3:23, KJV). By clothing the prodigal son in a robe, the father is not merely addressing his son's physical vulnerability but also symbolically restoring the original glory that was lost.

Alongside the robe, the prodigal son is also adorned with a ring that symbolizes authority. In ancient times, rings were not solely decorative but carried significant meaning. The gift of a ring denotes trust, responsibility, and the granting of authority. By bestowing the ring upon his son, the father is not only welcoming him back into the family but also acknowledging his ability to participate actively in the affairs of the household. It signifies the father's trust in his son's potential and reaffirms his position within the family structure.

After we receive the Father's love, He clothes us with His glory. He envelops us with His presence. In today's world, where individuals are constantly searching for meaning and purpose, one can argue that the only thing that sets God's people apart from the people of the world is the presence of God. This is not a new concept; it has been discussed and emphasized throughout history by various Bible-based books and teachings. Moses, a faithful servant of God, understood the importance of God's presence. In verse 15 of Exodus chapter 33 (NASB), he responds to the Lord, saying, "If Your presence does not go with us, do not lead us up from here." Moses recognizes that without God's presence, there is no point in proceeding further. He deeply understands that the presence of God is what distinguishes His people from all the other inhabitants of the earth.

In verse 16 (NKJV), "For how then will it be known that Your people and I have found grace in Your sight, except You go with us? So, we shall be separate, Your people and I, from all the people who are upon the face of the earth."

Moses truly understood the importance of God's presence in the lives of His children. Why is God's presence so crucial? What does it mean for God's people? The presence of God represents His guidance, protection, provision, and all of Him. Without the presence, God's children are exposed to the enemy. When God is with His people, they can experience peace, rest, divine direction, and protection. In a world that is full of chaos and uncertainty, the presence of God brings stability and peace.

The Tangibility of His Presence

There is a depth and richness to God's presence that cannot be fully grasped with words alone. It is a deeply personal and intimate encounter that defies explanation. It is as if the divine presence reaches out and touches us in a way that we can only feel and not fully comprehend or have a vocabulary to express it. It is a powerful and tangible force that engulfs us, surrounding us with an undeniable sense of His divinity. Words fall short when attempting to capture the sheer magnitude and grandeur of this Presence. It is an experience that must be felt to truly comprehend its depth and significance. While encounters with the Holy Spirit are deeply personal, they often have lasting effects on individuals, churches, and communities. You can never come in contact with God's presence and remain the same. An encounter with the Holy Spirit is a profound and transformative experience that defies explanation.

This reminds me of a time when a friend came to spend the night with me back then. Little did I know that this ordinary evening would turn into a life-transforming event for him. I only had a twin-size bed in my room, so I offered him my bed, and I slept on a small mat on the floor. Those were the days of humble beginnings, yet I would not trade the sweet times I had with the Holy Spirit during that stage of my life for anything.

I woke up from a deep sleep in the quiet of the night to see my friend awake and in tears. He sat up in the bed; he couldn't sleep. In utter amazement, I asked why he was crying, and he started to describe something I had felt so many times. An inexplicable beauty had surrounded him. A presence that he couldn't quite put into words. At that moment, it became apparent that the Holy Spirit had stepped into the room. His presence was so strong in the room that night. I sat on the mat, knowing what was going on. I began to pray in whispers, acknowledging the presence of the Holy Spirit. Telling Him how much we love Him and how much we need Him. This experience lasted for hours; I had to plead literally that the presence be lifted so my friend could sleep that night. This was in my early days of experiencing the Holy Spirit, and I didn't know better back then; I would have allowed Him to fully accomplish what He came to do in my friend, even if it meant a sleepless night for either of us.

For my friend, that encounter with the Holy Spirit was a turning point in his life. He didn't consider himself a serious believer prior to this event, so this was all strange to Him. Even though he knew something was different, he was short of words to describe his experience. His intended one-night stay with me turned to three days. In fact, he did not want to leave, but I had to assure him that he could have the same experience anywhere. The Holy Spirit is not limited to a particular location. We can experience Him whenever we yield to Him. My friend went back to a changed individual. Glory be to God!

From time immemorial, man has sought to understand and connect with this divine presence. Throughout history, countless scriptures, Christian books, and teachings have been written in an attempt to describe this physical manifestation of God's presence. Yet, it remains elusive, transcending human comprehension. It is a physical manifestation; it is an awe-inspiring experience. It transcends the confines of our physical world. It is an encounter with something beyond ourselves, a connection to a higher power that cannot be explained by reason alone or by using descriptions of things in our ephemeral realm. It exists beyond the realm of human comprehension, challenging our limited capacity for knowledge and understanding. The absence of words to adequately describe this presence highlights its ineffable nature.

It is like warmth and peace enveloping you in real-time. It is an intense yet comforting touch that leaves no room for doubt. In the presence of God, all worries and fears dissipate, replaced by a deep sense of peace and joy beyond description. When God's presence dwells within a person's life, everything changes. It is in His presence that one can find true rest, peace, and fulfillment. The desire for sin and worldly pleasures pale in comparison to the desire for His presence. God's presence brings a sense of purpose and direction that surpasses any worldly pursuit. It is a transformative experience that sets one apart from the people of the world.

The presence of God brings about a life that is marked by love, grace, and compassion. When God's presence dwells within an individual, it enables them to love and care for others in a way that is supernatural. It allows them to extend forgiveness, show kindness, and offer hope to those around them. This is what truly sets God's people apart from the people of the world—their ability to exemplify God's character and reflect His love to others. The presence of God brings peace, stillness, and stability in the face of chaos and the challenges of life. Oh, how I pray that you, the reader, will desire such and have a taste of this precious experience!

The presence of God also brings favor and blessings to His people. In verse 16 of Exodus 33 (NKJV), Moses says, "For how then can it be known that Your people and I have found favor in Your sight unless You go with us?" God's presence distinguishes His people and marks them as recipients of His favor. This favor opens doors, provides opportunities, and brings about supernatural blessings that are beyond human comprehension. The presence of God transforms and changes His people. In the presence of God, hearts are softened, minds are renewed, and lives are transformed. When His presence fills a space, His glory radiates, leaving a lasting impact on those who encounter it.

Under Old and New Covenants

In the Old Testament, the presence of God was often represented by the Ark of the Covenant, which symbolized God's dwelling among His people. The Ark signified the tangible presence of God in the midst of His chosen nation. It was a constant reminder that they were different and set apart from the surrounding nations.

The Ark was housed in the Tabernacle, the dwelling place of God's presence among the Israelites during their journey in the wilderness. It was a constant reminder to the people that God was with them, leading and protecting them. Priests carried the Ark during their battles, and it was crucial to numerous military victories. The presence of the Ark symbolized God's glory and authority. It was revered as a powerful symbol of the covenant between God and His people. The Israelites believed it to be a tangible representation of God's presence among them, and it held a prominent place in their worship.

In the New Testament, we see a shift in how God's presence is experienced. Jesus, God's Son, came to earth to reconcile humanity to God. He promised His disciples that after His departure, He would send the Holy Spirit to be with them forever. The Holy Spirit would not dwell in an external object like the Ark but would reside within the hearts of believers. The Holy Spirit has a transformative role in the lives of believers. He empowers and equips them, guiding them in their spiritual journeys. Through the Holy Spirit, believers experience God's presence on a personal and intimate level. They no longer need an external representation like the Ark; they have the indwelling presence of the Holy Spirit. However, we should not diminish the significance of the Ark of the Covenant. It served as a foreshadowing of what was to come in the New Testament. Just as the Ark represented God's presence among the Israelites, the Holy Spirit represents God's presence within believers. The Ark was a physical symbol; the Holy Spirit is a spiritual reality. Glory to God!

The Manifest Presence of God

It is important to note that God's presence is not exclusive to a specific location or building. It is not limited to the walls of a church or the confines of a sacred space.

The psalmist declares,

> Where can I go from your Spirit? Where can I flee from your presence? If I go up to the heavens, you are there; if I make my bed in the depths, you are there. If I rise on the wings of the dawn, if I settle on the far side of the sea, even there your hand will guide me, your right hand will hold me fast.
>
> Psalm 139:7–10 (NIV)

These verses depict the omnipresence of God. There is no place in the universe where God's presence is not felt. However, the psalmist also acknowledges that there are times when God's presence becomes experiential or manifest. In these moments, God unveils Himself to the individual in a tangible and powerful way.

Manifest presence is not simply a theological concept; it is a deeply personal and transformative experience. When someone encounters the manifest presence of God, they are overwhelmed by His holiness, His love, and His power. It is a moment of transcendence, where the finite encounters the infinite. It is important to note that God's manifest presence is not something that can be conjured or manufactured by human efforts. It is a divine revelation that is entirely dependent on God's sovereign will. God chooses to reveal Himself in His own time in various degrees and in His own way. As human beings, we can only position ourselves in a posture of humility and openness, inviting

God to make Himself known to us. God can reveal Himself to His people in a variety of settings and circumstances.

God's presence is available to everyone who seeks Him wholeheartedly. We can experience His presence in our homes, workplaces, and even in the midst of our daily routines. The presence of God sets His people apart not by their outward appearance or religious rituals but by the genuine relationship they have with Him. It is through an intimate relationship with God that His people can experience the life-transforming power of His presence and radiate such to the world around them.

Dear God, I pray that You visit this reader. Reveal Yourself through the presence of Your Spirit, bringing needed changes and transformation. Let them experience the transformative power of Your holy presence. Thank You, Holy Spirit.

CHAPTER 14
FELLOWSHIPPING WITH THE HOLY SPIRIT

Fellowshipping with the Holy Spirit has been a transformative journey for me. It is an experience that has deepened my understanding of God, enriched my spiritual growth, and brought me closer to the Father. Night after night, in the solitude of my room, the Holy Spirit has graciously chosen to reveal Himself to me, guiding me through the corridors of spiritual enlightenment and illuminating the Word of God. The Holy Spirit is our Advocate or Comforter. He is not the errand entity or the least among the Godhead. He is the One who brings forth guidance, wisdom, and understanding. We see Him throughout the Bible. He is powerful but gentle. As a devout believer, I have always sought to understand and enhance my relationship with the Holy Spirit. His presence has been a source of solace, inspiration, and empowerment in my life. The Holy Spirit's presence is not just an ethereal concept or a theological doctrine; it is a tangible reality that transforms lives and reveals the true depths of God's love. I have tasted His presence and felt His touch, and I can confidently say that nothing comes close. It is an unparalleled experience that ignites the soul and spurs it towards divine purpose. The presence of the Holy Spirit is everything.

One of the most profound aspects of my fellowship with the Holy Spirit is the way in which He manifests Himself. While the Holy Spirit is omnipresent, there is an overt sense of His tangible presence during those moments of personal devotion and communion. It is as if a gentle breeze caresses my being, reminding me of His constant companionship. During these intimate encounters, the Holy Spirit unravels the depths of Scripture and imparts divine wisdom and revelation to my heart and mind. He breathes life into the written word, transforming it into a living and active force within my life. The Holy Spirit has been my ultimate instructor, patiently guiding me through the complexities of Scripture, unraveling its truths, and revealing its hidden treasures. He helps us discern the areas of our lives that require transformation, urging us to walk in righteousness and godliness.

No religious experience could compare to the intimacy of the Precious Holy Spirit. The Holy Spirit's presence transcended the boundaries of earthly establishments. I won't trade my relationship with the Holy Spirit for anything. In my fellowship with Him, my prayers have gained new depths. The Holy Spirit intercedes on my behalf, translating the deepest longings of my heart into petitions before the throne of God. He aligns my desires with the will of God and imparts a sense of peace and assurance, knowing that my prayers are heard.

Just like the experience I shared at the beginning of this book, the Holy Spirit transformed my worship. As I lift my voice in adoration and surrender, the Holy Spirit empowers my praises, transforming them into a sweet aroma before the throne of God.

Through His presence, my worship transcends the realm of the physical and enters the spiritual, connecting me intimately with my Creator.

Beyond the personal benefits of my fellowship with the Holy Spirit, I have also witnessed the transformative power of this communion in the lives of others. I have seen a great transformation in my wife and our children. The Holy Spirit equips Christians for service and ministry with spiritual gifts. He ignites a passion for evangelism, compelling believers to share the life-transforming message of the Gospel with boldness and conviction.

As Christians, we have been blessed with the indwelling presence of the Holy Spirit. He is not a distant force or an abstract concept but a divine being who desires to commune with us in a personal and intimate way. Developing fellowship with the Holy Spirit involves opening our hearts to His presence, listening to His guidance, and experiencing the transformative power of His love in our lives. Fellowship with the Holy Spirit begins with acknowledging His role in our lives and embracing His presence as a constant companion. He is our helper, our comforter, and our guide. Just as we would seek companionship with a close friend, we can intentionally cultivate a relationship with the Holy Spirit. It involves recognizing His presence in every moment, inviting Him into our thoughts, decisions, and actions, and being attentive to His gentle nudges and promptings.

Listening to the Holy Spirit is an essential aspect of fellowship. He speaks to us in various ways—through a still, small voice, through Scripture, through godly counsel, or through circumstances, through vision, dreams, and many more. To listen to the Holy

Spirit, we need to cultivate a heart of surrender and attentiveness. It requires quieting the noise around us, being receptive to His leading, and discerning His voice amidst the distractions of life. The more we practice listening, the more attuned we become to His presence and the clearer His guidance becomes.

The Holy Spirit desires to guide us in every area of our lives, from making decisions to navigating relationships to living out our calling. By intentionally seeking His guidance and relying on His wisdom, we can experience His direction and experience a deeper sense of purpose and fulfillment. As we yield to His work within us, He manifests divine qualities such as an overflowing abundance of love, an exuberant joy that knows no bounds, a profound peace that surpasses all understanding, and an unwavering patience that endures through every trial. A genuine kindness that radiates like a beacon of light, an impeccable goodness that shines forth in every action, an unyielding faithfulness that remains steadfast in the face of adversity, a gentle spirit that soothes and heals the wounded soul, and a resolute self-control that empowers one to conquer every temptation. These fruits of the Spirit not only impact our own lives but also influence our relationships and interactions with others. It is the Holy Spirit who performs the most magnificent transformation within us, starting from the depths of our very being and radiating outwards. Just as a glorious sunrise illuminates the sky, the Holy Spirit illuminates our souls, molding us into the likeness of our precious Savior, Jesus Christ. Through His divine power, we are empowered to mirror the very essence of His character, shining brightly for all to see in this world. Hallelujah!

Understanding the Role and Work of the Holy Spirit

As human beings, we often struggle to comprehend the fullness of the Holy Spirit's role and work in our lives. The Holy Spirit is not merely an abstract concept or a distant force but a divine person—a member of the triune God who desires to have a personal relationship with us.

To better understand the role and work of the Holy Spirit, we can explore His attributes, His functions, and the ways in which He impacts our lives. The Holy Spirit is our helper, our comforter, and our advocate. He comes alongside us in our journey of faith, offering guidance, wisdom, and support. Just as a trusted friend walks with us through life's joys and challenges, the Holy Spirit walks with us every step of the way. He is the One who brings us comfort in times of sorrow, peace in times of anxiety, and strength in times of weakness. The Holy Spirit is our constant companion, providing the assistance we need to navigate life's complexities.

One of the primary roles of the Holy Spirit is to reveal truth to us. Through His presence, the Holy Spirit illuminates the Scriptures, opening our hearts and minds to understand God's Word. He guides us into a deeper understanding of God's character, His purposes, and His ways.

It is through the Holy Spirit's work that we can grasp the truth of the Gospel, comprehend God's love and grace, and grow in our knowledge of God's will for our lives. The Holy Spirit also convicts us of sin, righteousness, and judgment (John 16:8–11). He brings to light areas in our lives that are not aligned with God's standards, convicting us of our need for repentance and leading us toward righteousness. His conviction is not meant to condemn or shame us but to bring about genuine repentance and restoration. By the power of the Holy Spirit, we are led on a path of sanctity and uprightness, allowing us to mirror the very essence of Christ's nature (Philippians 1:11).

Furthermore, the Holy Spirit graciously bestows upon us the divine empowerment required for service and ministry. He equips us with spiritual gifts, enabling us to fulfill the unique calling God has placed upon our lives, whether it be the noble act of teaching, the humble act of serving, the uplifting act of encouraging, or any other divine gift bestowed upon us. It is the Holy Spirit who graciously endows us with the power to faithfully serve our Almighty God and edify the sacred body of Christ. It is by the empowering of the Holy Spirit that we are able to produce fruit in our lives and leave a beneficial influence on the world around us. The Holy Spirit is also involved in the process of our spiritual transformation. He works within us to conform us to the image of Christ, renewing our minds and regenerating our hearts. He empowers us to overcome the desires of the flesh and to live according to the Spirit. It is through the Holy Spirit's sanctifying work that we are continually being molded into the likeness of Christ, growing in love, joy, peace, patience, kindness, goodness, faithfulness, gentleness, and self-control.

The Holy Spirit is the unifying force within the body of Christ. He brings together diverse believers, forming a unified community where each member contributes their unique gifts and talents. Through the Holy Spirit's work, we are united in Christ, connected as one body, and empowered to love and serve one another. It is through the Holy Spirit's presence that we experience the beauty of genuine fellowship and unity. In order to fully grasp the role and work of the Holy Spirit, we must maintain a posture of openness and surrender. We must keep an open relationship with Him, inviting Him to have full access to our lives. As we yield to His leading, rely on His strength, and allow Him to work in and through us, we will experience the transformative power of the Holy Spirit in profound and life-changing ways.

May we embrace His guidance, comfort, and empowerment in our lives. And as we yield to the work of the Holy Spirit, may we be transformed into the image of Christ, united in fellowship with one another, and empowered to fulfill the purposes of God in the world.

Deepening Relationship and Communion with the Spirit

We long for deep and meaningful relationships. We desire to connect with others on a deep level. We want to be understood and to experience a sense of belonging. This longing also extends to our relationship with the Holy Spirit. Just as we nurture our relationships with friends and loved ones, we can actively pursue a deepening relationship and communion with the Holy Spirit. Deepening our relationship and communion with the Holy Spirit starts with an intentional desire and hunger for His presence. It involves recognizing Him as a person, as a divine being with whom we can have a personal and intimate connection. We must approach our relationship with the Holy Spirit with the same sincerity, attentiveness, and commitment as we would in any human relationship.

A crucial aspect of growing our relationship and communion with the Holy Spirit is spending dedicated time in prayer and worship. Just as we invest time and effort into building relationships with others, we must set aside time to engage in intimate conversation and worship with the Spirit. Through prayer, we pour out our hearts, express our love and adoration, and seek His guidance and wisdom. Through worship, we create an environment where His presence is magnified, and our hearts are tuned to His voice. Developing a habit of listening to the Holy Spirit is vital in strengthening our communion with Him. It requires creating space for silence and stillness, allowing us to hear His gentle whispers and promptings. Many believers are in haste when they come to the presence of God. They want answers to their prayers immediately. They want God to speak fast and act fast because of their busy schedules. The Bible tells us not to leave the presence of God in haste. "Do not be hasty to go from his presence. Do not take your stand for an evil thing, for he does whatever pleases him" (Ecclesiastes 8:3, NKJV). God is the King of the whole universe. He will do what pleases Him. He speaks when He desires to. Therefore, you must learn to be still in His presence.

Cultivating Awareness of His Nearness

Because we are human beings, we often separate the spiritual from the mundane, but God invites us to practice His presence in every aspect of our lives. This begins with a shift in mindset, recognizing that God is with us at all times. We may believe in His existence but fail to fully grasp the reality of His nearness and presence in our lives. However, God is not distant or detached from us; He desires an intimate relationship with us and longs for us to be aware of His nearness.

Cultivating awareness of God's nearness begins with a shift in our perspective—a conscious decision to believe that He is always present with us. It is acknowledging that He is not a far-off deity but a loving Father who walks beside us every step of the way. This shift in perspective allows us to see the signs of His presence in the everyday moments of our lives.

One way to cultivate awareness of His nearness is through the practice of silence. Taking intentional moments of quietude allows us to tune in to God's presence in the midst of our busy lives. It is in the moments of silence that we can hear His gentle whispers, feel His comforting embrace, and sense His guiding hand. By intentionally creating space for stillness, we open ourselves to a deeper awareness of His nearness.

Another practice is paying attention to the signs of God's presence in our daily experiences. It involves being attuned to the small miracles, answered prayers, and moments of divine guidance that often go unnoticed. By being present and observant, we can recognize God's fingerprints in the beauty of nature, the kindness of others, or the unexpected blessings that come our way. Cultivating awareness of His nearness involves training our hearts and minds to see the ways He is actively at work in our lives.

Communion of the Holy Spirit

Experiencing the presence of God in daily life begins with acknowledging God's constant presence and inviting Him into our daily routines. Whether during our morning commute, a conversation with a colleague, or while doing household chores, we can train ourselves to be aware of His nearness and seek to encounter Him in every situation.

One of the ways to experience the presence of God in our daily life is through the study and reflection on His Word—the Bible. In the Scriptures, we encounter the living words of God, and as we immerse ourselves in His truth, we open ourselves to His presence and guidance. Each passage becomes an opportunity to hear God's voice, to gain wisdom for the challenges we face, and to experience His love and grace anew. Through the Scriptures, God speaks directly into our lives, bringing comfort, conviction, and revelation. The Bible talks about Samuel and how he encounters God daily through the Word of God. "The LORD continued to appear at Shiloh, and there he revealed himself to Samuel through his word" (1 Samuel 3:21, NIV).

Prayer is a powerful means of experiencing the presence of God. It is an ongoing conversation with our Heavenly Father—a constant connection that allows us to pour out our hearts, seek His guidance, and listen to His gentle whisper. In prayer, we invite God into our daily concerns, joys, and struggles, knowing that He is attentive to our every word. Contrary to what we may think, God is not trying to endure our time with Him. As a good Father, He longs for our time of communing with Him. Through this intimate exchange, we can experience His peace, receive His comfort, and discern His leading in our lives.

Experiencing the presence of God in daily life also involves being attuned to the movement of His Spirit within us. The Holy

Spirit dwells within every believer, offering guidance, conviction, and empowerment. By cultivating a sensitivity to the Spirit's prompting, we can discern His leading in decision-making, experience His comfort in times of distress, and receive His power to live in alignment with God's will. At times, we may receive His prompting, a small nudge to come away with Him. To fellowship with Him. These moments are to be heeded and hallowed. I've had such moments in the middle of watching a movie with my family or doing other things. I would excuse myself and find a quiet place to be with Him. I've also learned to be alone with Him even in the middle of a noisy environment by tuning out the external stimuli and yielding to His voice within me. It is through the Spirit's work within us that we can truly experience the transformative presence of God in our daily lives. Our daily experiences become sacred encounters, and our hearts are filled with awe and gratitude for the privilege of walking in communion with our Heavenly Father.

Cultivating a Vibrant Prayer Life

Prayer is a powerful and transformative practice that allows us to commune with our Heavenly Father, seek His guidance, and experience His presence. Having a vibrant prayer life is an ongoing journey—a dance of vulnerability, persistence, and surrender. It is an invitation to deepen our intimacy with God and align our hearts with His purposes. As human beings, we can embrace certain principles to foster a vibrant prayer life and experience its richness.

Firstly, consistency is key. Just as a plant requires regular watering to thrive, our prayer life flourishes when we make it a daily habit. It is essential to carve out a dedicated time each day to be alone with God, to pour out our hearts, and to listen to His voice. Whether in the morning, afternoon, or evening, finding a time that works best for us and committing to it helps to cultivate a consistent and vibrant prayer life. This nurtures the connection we have with Him.

In addition to consistency, creating a sacred space for prayer enhances our experience. It can be a quiet corner of our home, a peaceful garden, or any place where we feel a sense of calm, void of distractions. By intentionally setting apart a physical space for prayer, we create an atmosphere conducive to communing with Him. This sacred space becomes a sanctuary where we can retreat and focus our hearts and minds on His presence. A time when we can pour out our joys, sorrows, dreams, and worries, knowing that He hears and cares for every word we utter.

To foster a vibrant prayer life, it is crucial to approach prayer with an attitude of humility and surrender. Recognizing our dependence on God, we come before Him with open hands, offering our desires, dreams, and plans in surrender to His will. We lay down our agendas and align ourselves with His purposes, trusting that His ways are higher and His plans are perfect. This posture of surrender invites Him to work in and through us, allowing His power to be made manifest in our lives.

A vibrant prayer life is nurtured through a posture of gratitude. By cultivating a heart of thanksgiving, we acknowledge God's faithfulness, goodness, and provision in our lives. Expressing gratitude in prayer helps shift our focus from our own needs and concerns to recognizing and appreciating the blessings and answered prayers we have received. Gratitude opens our hearts to a more profound experience of God's love and fosters inner contentment and joy.

In our quest to cultivate a vibrant prayer life, seeking guidance from God's Word is essential. The Bible serves as a wellspring of wisdom, encouragement, and inspiration for our prayers. Through the Scripture, we gain insight into God's character, His promises, and His desires for us. Meditating on His Word equips us with the right language to express our prayers, shapes our understanding of who He is, and aligns our desires with His heart. By knowing His Word, we can become familiar with His ways, plans, and promises for us. This enables us to pray according to His will and gives assurance that our petitions will be granted according to the promises in His Word (1 John 5:14).

Lastly, cultivating a vibrant prayer life thrives in the context of community. Joining fellow believers in prayer, participating in prayer groups or prayer partnerships, and sharing our prayer requests and praises with others strengthens our spiritual journey. The support, accountability, and encouragement of a faith community uplift and invigorate our prayer life, reminding us that we are not alone in our pursuit of intimacy with God. As human beings, we have the privilege of cultivating a vibrant prayer life—a life marked by consistent communion with our Heavenly Father, a heart posture of surrender and gratitude, and an openness to His transformative work within us. May we embrace this invitation to a vibrant prayer life, trusting that as we draw near to God in prayer, He will draw near to us (James 4:8). May our prayers become a wellspring of connection, transformation, and intimacy with our loving Heavenly Father.

CHAPTER 15
CARRIERS OF GOD'S PRESENCE

As human beings, we often long for a deeper sense of connection with God's presence in our daily lives. We desire to encounter Him not only in moments of worship or prayer but in the ordinary and mundane aspects of our existence. Thankfully, God's presence is not limited to specific times or sacred spaces. As believers who have been redeemed by the blood and filled with the Holy Ghost, we are carriers of God's divine presence. He desires to walk with us intimately in every moment, bringing comfort and guidance and transforming our ordinary experiences into extraordinary encounters. Not only that, but the carriers of God's presence also hold within them the potential to change the world. They possess the power to heal broken hearts, mend fractured relationships, and bring hope to the hopeless. Their very presence carries the fragrance of divine love, bringing warmth and comfort to those who have lost their way.

There Is a River

"There is a river whose streams make glad the city of God, the holy place where the Most High dwells" (Psalm 46:4, NIV). These words in the holy Scripture depict a powerful image of the divine presence of God. Throughout history, rivers have held significant symbolism in various cultures, representing life, renewal, and spiritual nourishment. The streams of this river serve as a constant reminder of the everlasting presence of God. Just as the flowing water nurtures the surrounding landscape, the streams of the city of God nourish the souls of its inhabitants, filling them with a profound sense of gladness and fulfillment. The river's gentle current washes away the burdens and worries of everyday life, providing peace to those who seek it.

In the book of Zechariah, we come across a promise from the Lord Himself. He declares, "I will return to Zion and dwell in Jerusalem" (Zechariah 8:3, NIV). This statement directly spoke to the Israelites, assuring them of God's presence and restoration. However, as believers in Christ, we can also apply this promise to ourselves as we become partakers of the new covenant through His sacrifice on the cross. Through the Scriptures, we understand that God's dwelling place is not confined to a physical location but resides within the hearts of His faithful followers.

The New Testament brings a perspective to the revelation of where God dwells. In his letter to the Corinthians, the apostle Paul enlightens us by saying, "Do you not know that your bodies are temples of the Holy Spirit, who is in you, whom you have received from God?" (1 Corinthians 6:19, NIV). This profound statement reveals the intimate union between God and the believers. As temples of the Holy Spirit, our bodies become sacred abodes for God. This truth is further emphasized in Paul's letter to the Ephesians, where he writes, "And in him you too are being built together to become a dwelling in which God lives by his Spirit" (Ephesians 2:22, NIV). Here, Paul highlights the collective nature of God's dwelling place. It is important to understand, as believers, that we are not isolated temples but are joined together in unity. This unity forms the body of Christ, and it is within this body that God chooses to reside.

The city of God, often referred to as the holy place, is a sacred space where the Most High dwells. It is a realm that transcends earthly limitations, where the divine essence permeates every aspect of existence. In this realm, love is the guiding force, and compassion reigns supreme. It is a place where all souls can find solace and refuge.

This river that makes glad the city of God is a powerful reminder of the transformative power of the divine presence of God. It signifies that the mere existence of this presence within our lives brings about a sense of joy and contentment that surpasses all worldly pleasures. Knowing that you carry God's divine presence brings peace that supersedes all understanding. You are not at war with yourself nor in competition with anyone. It is a reminder that true fulfillment comes not from external achievements or material possessions but from an inner connection with God.

In our fast-paced lives, it is easy to get caught up in the illusion of material success and earthly pursuits. We often forget to nurture our souls and seek refuge in the city of God. However, when we take the time to reconnect with God, we begin to live as we were created to be. The river of divine love and wisdom is always flowing, ready to bring solace, guidance, and profound gladness to our lives.

Holy Spirit: The River of Life

"He that believeth on me, as the scripture hath said, out of his belly shall flow rivers of living water" (John 7:38, KJV).

These powerful words from the Scripture hold deep meaning and offer profound insights into the transformative power of the Holy Spirit. To truly understand the essence of this scripture, we must first grasp the context in which it was spoken. These words were uttered by Jesus Christ Himself during a momentous occasion, the Feast of Tabernacles. This Jewish festival was a celebration of God's provision and a time of spiritual reflection and renewal. It was in this setting that Jesus spoke about the transformative power of faith. When Jesus referred to "believe on me" (John 7:38, KJV), He was referring to a deep, unwavering faith in Him as the Son of God. This belief goes beyond mere acknowledgment of His existence or recognition of His teachings. It involves absolute trust, surrender, and a personal relationship with Him.

The phrase "out of his belly shall flow rivers of living water" (John 7:38, KJV) carries profound symbolism. In biblical times, the belly was considered the seat of emotions and desires. It represented the depths of one's being, the core of one's identity. The flowing rivers of living water signify the person of the Holy Spirit. "But this He spoke concerning the Spirit, whom those believing in Him would receive; for the Holy Spirit was not yet given, because Jesus was not yet glorified" (John 7:39, NKJV).

The Holy Spirit is often associated with water in the Bible, symbolizing cleansing, refreshing, and renewal. Just as a river brings life and sustenance to the land it flows through, the Holy Spirit brings vitality and spiritual abundance to the believer.

When we believe in Jesus and receive the Holy Spirit, our lives are transformed. The stagnant and parched areas of our hearts are revitalized, and a river of living water begins to flow from within us. This river brings a deep sense of peace, joy, and purpose. It quenches our spiritual thirst and empowers us to live a life that honors and reflects the teachings of Jesus.

A Lifeless Desert

Over the past few years, Texas has experienced a heatwave that has had significant impacts on the environment and wildlife, causing various changes. Despite being accustomed to the weather, the temperature has risen considerably, setting new records as the hottest years ever recorded. These elevated temperatures have not only posed challenges for Texans but have also negatively affected plant life and aquatic species, particularly fish residing in lakes.

During one of my prayer walks, I visited a park that used to be a popular tourist spot. However, what I found was disheartening. The ground was littered with bones of dead fish and all kinds of water creatures. It was evident that the absence of fresh, flowing water had caused significant damage. People used to come to this place to admire the different species of fish, but now all the beauty is gone.

In that moment, the Lord spoke to me and made a profound revelation. He said that the same thing happens when His presence is absent in a gathering. The beauty of the church or any Christian gathering lies in the manifested presence of the Holy Spirit—the river of life among His people. How often do we organize events or gatherings for God without His presence being truly felt? How often do we prepare a table of worship, but the object of our worship is absent? People labor and serve tirelessly but end up feeling tired and worn out. It is the Holy Spirit that gives life and vitality to every aspect of our lives. There are works that produce life, and there are works that lead to spiritual death and bankruptcy. The honest question is, why do we do what we do? The lack of the glorious presence of God among His people has resulted in the uprising of an unhealthy competitive spirit that is rampaging among brethren.

In Ezekiel 47:9 (NKJV), it is written, "And it shall be that every living thing that moves, wherever the rivers go, will live. There will be a very great multitude of fish because these waters go there; for they will be healed, and everything will live wherever the river goes." This verse beautifully illustrates the power and significance of the Holy Spirit. Just as fish thrive in flowing water, every living thing flourishes in the presence of the Holy Spirit.

Without the Holy Spirit, our gathering can be compared to a dry and lifeless desert. We may go through the motions, but the true essence of spiritual life is absent. Our efforts become tiresome and lack impact. People come to church but leave the service feeling more tired than when they came, or at best, they feel emotionally high from all the activities, but their spirit is shriveling up and dying within them. However, when we open ourselves up to the presence of the Holy Spirit, our gatherings become like an oasis in the desert, abounding with life and vibrancy—a place where dry bones come alive again.

> Because the palaces shall be forsaken; the multitude of the
> city shall be left; the forts and towers shall be for dens forever,

a joy of wild asses, a pasture of flocks; Until the spirit be poured upon us from on high, and the wilderness be a fruitful field, and the fruitful field be counted for a forest.

Isaiah 32:14–16 (KJV)

In a world that is often filled with despair and hopelessness, the Holy Spirit is the source of comfort, strength, and guidance. He is the river of life that can quench our thirst and satisfy the deepest longings of our souls. In Him, we find a refuge, a place of peace and restoration. The river of the Holy Spirit not only brings life to the individual but also to the collective body of believers. When the Holy Spirit is present, relationships are restored, divisions are mended, and unity prevails. The river of the Holy Spirit empowers us to love one another unconditionally, to serve selflessly, and to contribute to the growth of the church.

As believers, it is vital for us to recognize that we carry a life-changing power that emanates from God's presence. It is not a responsibility to be taken lightly, for the power we carry has the potential to heal the sick, mend broken hearts, and bring light to the darkest corners of society. It is a power that transcends human limitations and brings hope, healing, and restoration to a broken world. The power can break yokes, break curses, liberate the oppressed, and bring the life of God to our generation.

This power is not reserved exclusively for the elites; rather, it resides within every believer who chooses to embrace and embody the presence of God. We are not merely carriers of God's presence; we are carriers of His love, His redemption, and His power. The same power that worked in the lives of the apostles resides within us, empowering us to carry out the great commission of making disciples of all nations. It is not a power to be hoarded or kept to ourselves but a power to be shared and poured out onto others.

"For the earnest expectation of the creation eagerly waits for the revealing of the sons of God" (Romans 8:19, NKJV). Those in whom the power of divinity dwells. As carriers of God's presence, we are not called to parade our spirituality or impress one another with our feats. Rather, our purpose is to direct the radiance of this power toward the world that is dying of spiritual thirst. We understand that the responsibility placed upon us by this divine commission is greater than any personal gain or gratification.

To be a carrier of God's presence is not a title. It is a privilege that must not be taken lightly; it is not an exclusive club for the perfect or the pious. It is a calling extended to sons and daughters of the Heavenly Father who are willing to surrender their lives, fears, desires, and ambitions to the Holy Ghost and allow the power of God to flow through them. It is through this surrender that they are transformed, becoming vessels of light in a darkened world.

As carriers of God's presence, you possess the transformative ability to make a real difference in the lives of others and in the world as a whole. It is a calling that extends beyond personal comfort and self-gratification. It is a summons to be a beacon of hope, a living testament to the goodness and mercy of God. It is through our actions, words, and the very essence of our being that we are able to reveal the love of God to those who desperately need it. It is not a mere badge of honor or an opportunity to showcase your spirituality but a divine responsibility to extend God's love and grace to every corner of the earth. Just as the fish in the lakes of Texas depend on the life-giving flow of fresh water, so do we depend on the Holy Spirit to bring us to life.

So, let us not become complacent in our roles as carriers of God's presence. Let us actively seek ways to manifest His power in our daily lives, shining brightly in a world filled with darkness. Let us be intentional in extending His love and grace to those around us, knowing that we have been entrusted with a responsibility that has the potential to change lives, bring healing, and transform nations. Let us embrace our role with humility, reverence, and a burning passion to make a real difference in this world, for we are the carriers of God's presence, and the world is eagerly awaiting our manifestation.

CHAPTER 16

LONGING FOR MORE

"O God, You are my God; Early will I seek You; My soul thirsts for You; My flesh longs for You In a dry and thirsty land Where there is no water" (Psalm 63:1, NKJV).

These powerful words, penned by an ancient psalmist, resonate deeply with those who seek solace and fulfillment in their spiritual journey. It speaks of a desperate yearning, a craving for a God who alone can offer solace and quench the thirst of the soul. In another Psalm, he described the longing of his soul after God as that of a deer panting after the water (Psalm 42:1). Often, we find ourselves lost in the hustle and bustle of our everyday lives, consumed by our relentless pursuit of materials and success. Yet, beneath the surface, there lies an emptiness that cannot be filled by any worldly possessions or achievements. These moments call for us to turn our gaze towards God, seeking solace and purpose in His eternal arms.

Reading this verse, one may think of a deer that is just thirsty and in need of water to quench its everyday thirst. However, a deer will naturally pant and look for water after being chased by a hunter or a predator. Deers pant and need water to survive after being overheated. Without it, they become weak, vulnerable, and incapable of fulfilling their purpose in the natural order.

Similarly, just as the deer's survival is dependent on water, our souls are dependent on a connection with God to thrive and find fulfillment in times of despair when faced with the heat of the situations around us. This yearning is not irrational or baseless; rather, it emerges from a deep understanding of our limitations as human beings. We are finite beings bound by the constraints of time and space. Yet, within us resides a longing to be reunited with our Creator. Ecclesiastes 3:11 (NIV) brought some light into this when He said, "…He has also set eternity in the human heart; yet no one can fathom what God has done from beginning to end." Nothing in this world will ever satisfy the longing in the souls of men. It is a thirst that cannot be quenched by worldly pursuits or achievements.

Jesus, in Matthew chapter 11, verse 28 (KJV), gave an open invitation to every weary soul. He said, "Come unto Me….and I will give you rest." There is no other place to find rest but in Him alone. He also said in verse 6 of Matthew chapter 5 (NIV), "Blessed are those who hunger and thirst after righteousness for they will be filled." This confirms that there is a blessing reserved for those who hunger and thirst after God. He will not turn such away. They will be filled and satisfied.

Jesus also addressed this when speaking with the woman at the well in John chapter 5. In this account, we see Jesus offering this woman a different type of water. One that she had never heard of. A water that will keep someone from feeling thirsty. She must have walked miles to come to the outskirts of the city to draw water. This reminds me of my experience growing up. We did not have access to tap water, and we would wake up very early in the mornings and walk miles to the stream to fetch clean water for the house for cooking and drinking. We did this on most mornings before getting ready for school. Carrying those heavy pots on a long walk back home was not an easy task at all. I'm so thankful for the advent of boreholes and tap water!

I can imagine the Samaritan woman's excitement when she hears of water that will relieve her of this burden. She immediately asked for the water. However, Jesus pointed out to her that what He's offering her is more than water from a well she will have to go out to draw from. She would no longer have to travel to the physical well because the water that Jesus gives will become a never-drying fountain of water within her. Better yet, this fountain springs up into everlasting life. Hallelujah!

This longing for God is not merely a fleeting emotion or a passing desire. It is a deep-seated yearning that persists even in the face of adversity and challenges. It is a thirst that cannot be quenched by anything other than the presence of God Himself. "There is a path which no fowl knoweth, And which the vulture's eye hath not seen: The lion's whelps have not trodden it, Nor the fierce lion passed by it" (Job 28:7–8, KJV). Job is telling us that there is a secret place known and available only to a select few. Only when God's children step into this sacred place does God's power start to work for them.

Deep Calls unto the Deep

In verse 7 of Psalm 42, David continues his discourse about his longing for God. The search for God is not a passive act; it requires an active engagement of both the heart and the mind.

It entails a willingness to seek and explore the vast expanse of spiritual wisdom that exists in our God alone, for in Him lies all the treasures of wisdom and knowledge. However, this is only reserved for the seekers. Those who have gone deeper in intimacy with Him to know the mystery of God, namely Christ (Colossians 2:3). Seeking God wholeheartedly demands a commitment to death to self, death to the wisdom of this world to peel back the layers of our ego and connect with the great *I am*. The path towards God is not always easy. We may find ourselves wandering in a dry and weary land, encountering obstacles and challenges that test our faith. People may misunderstand our intentions. You may even be ridiculed sometimes. You may face distractions from every angle. Yet, it is in these moments of darkness that the longing for God becomes even more intense as that of the deer panting after water when chased by a predator. While going through our struggles and hardships, we find strength through the Holy Spirit to continue seeking God and to strive for a deeper connection with Him. He is our helper along the Christian journey. He strengthens us as we face opposition and challenges that arise to discourage us. It is important to mention that as you make up your mind to follow God, the enemy is also determined to do all it takes to stop you. However, we are more than conquerors through Christ. In Ephesians, chapter 3, verse 16, the apostle Paul prayed for the Ephesian Christians that they would be strengthened with might by the Holy Spirit in their inner man. This is what gives us spiritual stamina in our pursuit of intimacy with God.

The journey of seeking God defies a straightforward explanation or description. It is a deeply personal experience that varies from individual to individual. Regardless of the form it takes, the longing for God is a call to seek something greater, to embark on a transformative journey of knowing God in an experiential way. "My ears had heard of you but now my eyes have seen you" (Job 42:5, NIV). At the core of this longing lies a recognition of our own limitations. We acknowledge that we are mere mortals in a vast and complex universe, with a yearning for something greater than ourselves. There is a depth in God that He is calling us into. No matter what your current spiritual level is, there is a deeper place in God for you.

"Those who go down to the sea in ships. Who do business on great waters. They see the works of the LORD. And His wonders in the deep" (Psalm 107:23–24, NKJV).

There is a dimension in God that is only found in the deep places in Him. His secrets are with those who love Him and are willing to pay the price of pursuing intimacy with Him. Those who would not give up when the billows of the raging sea are crashing over them. When the storms of life threaten to overpower them, they hold on tenaciously, determined not to give up, and look to the Holy Spirit for strength. At times, saying "Holy Spirit, help me" may be the only prayer you have enough strength to mutter. You can rest assured that He will carry you and not allow you to fall by the roadside as you continue to pursue God, making Him your ultimate reward in life and reason for living. This longing for God signifies our innate understanding that there is more to life than what meets the eye, that there is a divine presence that can bring solace and meaning to our existence—God.

CHAPTER 17
SEASONS OF PREPARATION

From the moment we are born, God has a specific plan and purpose for us. He wants us to grow and mature in our faith, character, and abilities to fulfill this plan. However, this maturing process is not always a smooth and effortless journey. It often involves a season of refinement—a time of challenges, trials, and hardships that God employs to shape and mold individuals into the form He intended. Just as a potter takes a lump of clay and molds it into a beautiful vessel, so does God take us and shape us through life's various experiences and circumstances. These experiences are not meant to break or destroy us but to refine and strengthen us. They are designed to draw out the best in us and to develop our character and qualities. It is in these moments of testing that we learn valuable lessons, acquire wisdom, and grow in our relationship with God.

The season of refinement is often uncomfortable and painful. It may involve periods of loneliness, rejection, or failure according to the human standard. We may question our purpose and feel discouraged or unsure of ourselves. But it is during these times that God is doing His best work in us. He is stripping away our self-reliance, pride, and selfishness and replacing them with humility, trust, and a deep dependence on Him.

It is important to remember that this season of refinement is not a punishment or a sign of God's disapproval. On the contrary, it is a sign of His love and commitment to our growth and development. Just as a parent disciplines their child out of love and a desire to see them mature, so does God refine us out of His deep love for us. He wants us to become more like Him. This is a requirement for intimacy with Him, for He is a holy God whose eyes cannot behold iniquity (Habakkuk 1:13). He wants to rid us of all impurities so that we can become the best version of ourselves through which His Divine purpose can be expressed and so that we can make a positive impact in the world.

Joseph Remained Faithfull

The story of Joseph in the Bible is a prime example of this season of refinement. Joseph was chosen by God to become a great leader and ruler, but before he could fulfill this role, he had to go through a time of preparation and refinement. He was sold into slavery by his own brothers, falsely accused of a crime, and spent years in prison. But through it all, Joseph remained faithful to God and trusted in His plan. We may wonder why God would allow such trials and tribulations. However, it was through these hard times that Joseph's character was further refined, his faith deepened, and his leadership qualities were honed. God used these challenging experiences to prepare Joseph for the role he was destined to play. In the end, Joseph's time of refinement led to his promotion and the fulfillment of God's plan for his life. He became the second-in-command in Egypt and was able to save his family, the land of Egypt, and the world of his time from famine. Joseph's story teaches us that even in the darkest moments of our lives, God is still working behind the scenes, orchestrating events for our good and His glory.

How to Navigate the Season of Refinement

When a season of refinement is misunderstood, it can become a tool in the hands of the enemy to discourage and distract us from pursuing God.

Before God uses anyone, there is always a season of preparation. This season requires endurance, faith, and a willingness to grow. It demands that we embrace the challenges and uncertainties that come our way, knowing that they serve a greater purpose. Through these seasons of refinement, God shapes us into the individuals He intends us to be, equipping us to fulfill our unique roles in His divine plan.

So, how do we navigate these seasons so that they will accomplish God's desired purpose in our lives? It begins with surrendering to God's will and trusting that He loves us and knows what is best for us (Proverbs 3:5–6; Jeremiah 29:11). This means relinquishing our desires for instant gratification and recognizing that true growth takes time. It means maintaining a perspective that extends beyond our immediate circumstances, understanding that the challenges we face today will one day contribute to His greater purpose. In our moments of uncertainty, we can find solace in knowing that God works all things together for the good of those who love Him (Romans 8:28).

The process of spiritual growth and maturity is not a solitary endeavor. It requires humility and a willingness to seek guidance and wisdom not only from God but also from others that He leads us. Just as iron sharpens iron, we, too, can learn and grow from the experiences and insights of those who have successfully overcome similar hurdles in their faith journey. Through fellowship, mentorship, and sharing our own stories, we gain a broader perspective and a deeper appreciation for the divine plan that intertwines our lives with others. This, however, should be led by the Holy Spirit because many have lost their dreams or prolonged their journey in life by sharing their dreams and spiritual experiences with the wrong people. Joseph's life is a good case study for this. Remember that not everyone will understand what God is up to in your life.

God Has Plans for All His Children

God's plan for growth and maturity extends to everyone, not a selected few. It encompasses all of His children regardless of their backgrounds, circumstances, or past mistakes. God wants each and every one of us to maximize our potential in Him. He provides us with the tools and resources we need and guides us through the stages of preparation. He encourages us to embrace the challenges and uncertainties that life brings because each step forward brings us closer to the maturity that He desires for us. This journey leads to a connection with Him on an intimate level. Sometimes, we may feel inadequate or insignificant in the scheme of things. It's important to remember that God has a purpose for every one of us, and He has equipped us with everything we need to fulfill His plan for our lives.

The apostle Paul carefully stated this in Ephesians 2:10 (NLT), "For we are God's masterpiece. He has created us anew in Christ Jesus, so we can do the good things he planned for us long ago." Just as a skilled craftsman carefully selects the materials and tools needed for a masterpiece, God has carefully chosen each aspect of our lives to shape us into the individuals He envisions. Our life experiences, both positive and negative, are all part of the refining process that leads us toward maturity. Like a delicate clay pot being molded on a potter's wheel, we are being shaped, molded, and transformed by the loving hands of our Heavenly Father. It is easy to shrink away from difficulties and become discouraged when things don't go as planned. However, as we press on and persevere, we gain a deeper understanding of God's unfailing love and His desire for us to grow and mature.

The seasons of preparation are essential in the journey towards maturity. Just as a seed requires time to germinate and grow before it can bear fruit, we, too, need time to develop and cultivate our spiritual lives. During these seasons, God provides opportunities for growth and learning, guiding us toward a more personal connection with Him. It is through seeking His wisdom and guidance that we discover our true identity and purpose. Maturity, in the context of God's plan, encompasses not only the development of our spiritual lives but also our emotional, mental, and physical well-being. God desires for us to live balanced and fulfilling lives. As we embark on this journey towards maturity, let us remember that we are not alone. We are part of a greater plan, a plan that connects us with all of God's children. Let us support, encourage, and love one another as we walk together toward the fulfillment of God's divine purpose.

It's All About God

In a world that often revolves around promoting ourselves and pursuing gain, it's easy to lose sight of what matters. We get so caught up in our desires and ambitions that we forget we're small parts of something much bigger and greater than any one of us. Ultimately, it all comes down to God. He deserves all the glory in everything. I was reminded of this truth during an event where I was invited to sing and minister. As I observed the person who was leading worship before my turn, I couldn't help but notice the incredible impact they were making. The presence of God was intense in the atmosphere. The Spirit of God was moving in a powerful way, touching hearts and transforming lives. I was in awe of the atmosphere that had been created, and I knew that this was why we were all there.

When the moderator approached me and informed me that it was my turn to take over, I hesitated. How could I come forward and disrupt the flow of what God was already doing? It didn't feel right to interrupt the beautiful work that was taking place before my eyes and inject my own ten minutes. So, I made a decision: I told the moderator to let the person continue and use my time. I wanted to honor the presence of God and allow His work to continue unhindered.

At that moment, I came to understand a vital truth—it's not about us. It's not about our talents, our skills, or our abilities. It's about surrendering ourselves to the will of God and allowing Him to work through us. It's about acknowledging that everything we have and everything we are is a gift from Him. We are merely vessels, conduits through which His love and grace can flow.

When we recognize that it's all about God, our perspective shifts, our focus moves away from our own desires and ambitions, and instead, we become consumed with seeking His will and His glory. We no longer strive for personal recognition or success; instead, we strive to be faithful vessels for God's purposes.

This shift in perspective brings about a profound sense of freedom. We are no longer bound by the pressures of striving for worldly achievements or the constant need for validation. Instead, we find contentment in simply fulfilling our role in God's story. We understand that our value and significance lie in being obedient to Him and allowing Him to work through us.

Furthermore, recognizing that it's all about God brings about a sense of humility. We understand that we are not the center of the universe, but rather, we are a small part of God's grand design. We also see other believers as co-heirs and laborers, thus eliminating the competitive spirit that is growing rapidly among us. We are humbled by the fact that He chooses to use imperfect vessels like us to accomplish His purposes. We recognize our dependence on Him and surrender ourselves to His guidance.

We must constantly resist the temptation to make it all about ourselves and humbly submit to God's will. He has the master plan. We are all one piece of the puzzle for the bigger picture. Sometimes, it's necessary to step aside and allow God's work to unfold without our interference. We are called to be faithful vessels, allowing His love and grace to flow through us, making a lasting impact on those around us. Let us remember that it's not about us but rather about God. So, let us surrender to His will and trust that the process of maturity will ultimately lead us to a fulfilled and purposeful life. One that makes us more like our Heavenly Father and brings us into intimacy with Him.

CHAPTER 18
WALKING IN THE ANOINTING

Walking in the anointing is one of the outcomes of intimacy with God. When we receive the anointing, we are not only covered by the power of God, but it also resides within us. This infusion of divine power enables us to operate in ways unimaginable, surpassing our own abilities and limitations. The anointing is not a mere symbol or representation; it is the tangible manifestation of God's presence and glory.

The Hebrew word for anointing is *mashach,* meaning "to rub in." It signifies the act of smearing or rubbing oil onto a person or object. The Greek word for anointing is *chrism,* which conveys the idea of "smearing or rubbing." Both these words paint a vivid picture of anointing as something that is not only applied externally but also absorbed and integrated within.

As human beings, we are called to live a life of purpose and impact. We long to make a difference, to fulfill the unique calling and destiny placed upon our lives. For Jesus to fulfill His assignment on earth, God had to anoint Him. The Bible talks about how God anointed Jesus of Nazareth with the Holy Ghost and with power: who went about doing good and healing all that were oppressed of the devil; for God was with Him (Acts 10:38). Whatever we are called to do, whether to give godly counsel to an individual in a little corner of the room or share the Gospel with millions of people on a global scale, we need the anointing of God.

When we talk about intimacy with God, we are referring to a closeness that goes beyond mere knowledge and understanding. It is a relationship that is built on trust and a deep sense of connection. It is in this place of intimacy that we are able to fully experience the presence and power of God, and it is from this place that the anointing flows. It is the result of a surrendered life, a life that willingly submits to the leading and guiding of the Holy Spirit.

The anointing is not limited to those in full-time ministry or those who hold positions of leadership. It is available to every believer who is willing to seek and pursue God with all their heart. It is not based on our abilities or qualifications but rather on our willingness to surrender our lives to Him and allow Him to work through us for His glory.

Walking in the anointing requires a deep level of consecration and surrender. It means laying down our own desires and ambitions and aligning ourselves with God's purposes and plans. In order for the power of the Holy Spirit to continually transform and flow through us, humility and teachability are necessary. As humans, we are susceptible to the dangers and pitfalls of power. Power without the presence of God can become a destructive force, leading to arrogance, pride, and self-centeredness. It can corrupt the very essence of an individual, turning them into an enemy. Therefore, it is vital to maintain that closeness with God to prevent the anointing from becoming a harmful force.

When we walk in the anointing, we become vessels that God can use to bring about His kingdom on earth. We become conduits of His love, grace, and power as we allow Him to work through us to touch and transform the lives of those around us. It is not about us but rather about Him and His purposes being fulfilled in and through us.

Anointing Breaks the Yoke

In Isaiah 10:27, it is prophesied that on a certain day, the yoke shall be destroyed because of the anointing. This verse highlights the significance and transformative power of the anointing.

In a world plagued by suffering and the bondage of the enemy, it is crucial to understand the importance of the anointing. Yokes are symbolic of the burdens, bondages, and limitations that the enemy imposes on individuals. They represent the chains that hinder us from living a life of freedom, joy, and purpose. Today, many are struggling with addictions; many are under demonic influence and attack, and many marriages are suffering today because the devil has infiltrated them. Both old and young are helpless under the chains of addictions and immoralities like a stream in our streets.

Sometimes, it may even be the limitation that we set on ourselves. Growing up as a child, I faced the challenge of stuttering. It felt as if my words were trapped within me, causing immense frustration and embarrassment. This speech impediment crippled my confidence and hindered me from expressing myself effectively in public. However, everything changed when I began to immerse myself in the fellowship of the Holy Spirit. Through my fellowship and connection with the Holy Spirit, the yoke of stuttering was miraculously broken, and I found myself speaking freely and with clarity.

This profound transformation was not only a personal milestone but also a testament to the power of the anointing. As the divine power of the anointing permeates our inner being, it carries the transformative ability to conquer spiritual strongholds and dismantle the chains that bind us. It also empowers us to fulfill our unique calling and destiny, allowing us to manifest our God-given talents, abilities, and gifts by aligning our works, passions, and ambitions with God's agenda.

Walking in the anointing is not a one-time event but a lifelong journey of growth and dependence on the Holy Spirit. It is a continuous surrender of our lives to His leading and an ongoing pursuit of intimacy with Him. As we walk in the anointing, we become vessels through which God's power and love flow, impacting our spheres of influence. Our lives become testimonies of God's goodness and grace, and we are positioned to partner with Him in His redemptive work in the world.

The Price of the Anointing

Have you ever wondered why certain individuals appear to possess a powerful anointing while others find it challenging to tap into this spiritual blessing? The reason behind this is quite simple. There is always a cost associated with receiving the anointing. The price for the anointing is high, and only a few are willing to pay it. To walk in the anointing, one must be prepared to make sacrificial choices and embrace the transformative process that accompanies it.

The concept of the anointing can be traced back to biblical times, where it played a pivotal role in the lives of prophets, priests, and kings. We saw it in the lives of the apostles as well. This divine power bestowed upon individuals was not freely given; rather, it demanded a great sacrifice.

"Any of you ministers can have what I have if you'll only pay the price." Those were the words of a woman who was greatly used by God before she passed into Glory. Kathryn Kuhlman spoke of the price she had paid for the anointing of God on her ministry and the secret to the power of the Holy Spirit that we saw manifested in her meetings. She talked about death to self, carrying the cross.

Jesus Himself described this principle when He declared, "Unless a grain of wheat falls into the ground and dies, it remains alone; but if it dies, it produces much grain" (John 12:24, NKJV). In essence, the anointing requires us to let go of our desires, ambitions, and comforts in order to be used by God in ways we could never imagine.

The price for the anointing involves a commitment to a continuous life of prayer and intimacy with God. In order to tap into this divine power, we must cultivate a deep and personal relationship with the One who anoints us. This requires setting aside dedicated time for prayer, studying the Word of God, and seeking His presence daily. It is through this relentless pursuit of God that we are able to experience His anointing flowing through us. It necessitates a willingness to embrace the refining process.

Just as gold is purified through fire, we must endure trials and challenges that refine our character and strengthen our faith. These refining moments may take the form of adversity, persecution, or even spiritual warfare. In the process of seeking God, some people may just dislike you. They may say unkind words about you behind you and even to your face. Yet, you must always respond with love. It is through these experiences that we are shaped into vessels fit for the anointing. It is through these trials that God molds us into instruments of His power and grace.

What Do You Want Most?

Walking in the anointing means dying to self. This means surrendering our will and allowing God to take control of our lives. Many believers sing I surrender all, but when God visits the altar of their hearts, there is no place for Him, but only for the idols they have embraced in the place of the Father. Walking in the anointing requires humility, obedience, and a radical shift in our priorities. With Abraham, it was his Isaac. David said in Psalm 73:25 (BSB), "Whom have I in heaven but You? And on earth I desire no one besides You." In Philippians 3:8 (KJV), Paul said, "I count all things but loss for the excellency of the knowledge of Christ Jesus my Lord: for whom I have suffered the loss of all things, and do count them but dung, that I may win Christ."

We must be willing to let go of our own desires and align ourselves with the will of God. This may involve sacrificing personal ambitions, material possessions, and even relationships that hinder our spiritual growth. God will not take second place. He will not share space with idols in your heart. Anything less than all, He won't take it. You must constantly seek to please Him in all things.

The Difference between King David and King Saul

One of the key distinctions between David and Saul lies in their treatment of the Ark of the Covenant. The Ark represents God's throne, power, and anointing and held a central position in the religious and political life of the Israelites. David understood the significance of the Ark and recognized that establishing it as the highest priority was paramount for a successful reign. His first act as a monarch was to gather the nation and ensure that God was recognized as the true King, not himself. In sharp contrast, Saul neglected the Ark and failed to prioritize its presence within his kingdom. The consequences of this oversight were dire, as Saul's reign ultimately lasted only twenty years, while David's bloodline persevered through the centuries, culminating in the Messiah sitting on His eternal throne.

King Saul

The biblical account reveals that Saul, consumed by his own ambitions, overlooked the spiritual implications of his role as king. The Ark remained in obscurity in a place called Kirjath Jearim for a prolonged period as the nation lamented the absence of the Lord's presence. "The Ark remained in Kiriath-jearim for a long time—twenty years in all. During that time all Israel mourned because it seemed the LORD had abandoned them" (1 Samuel 7:2, NLT). Saul's oversight manifested in a lack of God's anointing, power, and throne in his kingdom. His reign was overshadowed by a neglect of spiritual matters, accompanied by personal desires for power and glory.

Saul, unfortunately, epitomized selfishness and a lack of regard for God's honor and God's anointing upon his life. Throughout his reign, he allowed his ego to control his actions, leading to disastrous consequences for himself and his people. It is essential to examine Saul's behavior and choices to understand the extent of his selfishness and disregard for God's honor. One prime example of Saul's selfishness lies in his obsession with recognition and adoration. He craved the attention that came with his position as king and constantly sought validation from those around him. In moments of great significance, he prioritized his own honor over that of God.

This unfortunate tendency is evident in the story of Saul's encounter with the prophet Samuel. When Samuel confronted Saul about his disobedience to God's command to completely destroy the Amalekites, Saul was more concerned about his image than about following God's instructions. As Samuel confronted him, Saul pleaded, "I know I have sinned. But please, at least honor me before the elders of my people and before Israel by coming back with me so that I may worship the LORD your God" (1 Samuel 15:30, NLT).

In this plea, Saul revealed his self-centeredness. Instead of sincerely remorseful for his transgressions, he was primarily concerned with salvaging his reputation before the people and obtaining their praise. His actions displayed a lack of true repentance and a denial of responsibility for his disobedience.

Intimacy With God

Moreover, Saul's selfishness extended beyond his desire for recognition and praise. He also displayed a careless attitude towards God's honor. As king, he was entrusted with leading God's people and upholding His divine laws. However, Saul consistently made decisions that directly opposed God's commands, demonstrating his disregard for God's honor.

Another example of Saul's careless attitude towards God's honor was his rash decision to offer a sacrifice before going into battle. In a moment of impatience and fear, Saul took matters into his own hands and transgressed the authority and role that God had assigned to priests, showing no concern for the sacredness of the priestly office.

Saul's selfishness and disregard for God's honor were not limited to his actions but also extended to his attitude toward others. He often treated those around him poorly, displaying a lack of empathy and selflessness. This was particularly evident in his relationship with David, whom he regarded as a rival and enemy. Saul's jealousy and insecurity towards David clouded his judgment and led him to make cruel decisions. Instead of appreciating David's loyalty and skill, Saul schemed to eliminate him and become the sole focus of attention and admiration. His selfishness undermined his ability to lead God's people and ultimately resulted in his downfall.

King David

David, on the other hand, recognized the importance of seeking God's favor and placing Him at the center of his rule. He put God first in all things. Proverbs 3:6 (TLB) proclaims,

"In everything you do, put God first, and he will direct you and crown your efforts with success."

David recognized the importance of God's presence and was determined to bring the Ark back to Jerusalem. He gathered all the chosen men of Israel, a staggering thirty thousand, and embarked on a journey to retrieve the Ark of God. This event highlights David's deep faith and understanding of the significance of having God's presence among his people. David's decision to gather such a large number of men exemplifies the importance he placed on this endeavor. He understood that this act was not just a mere task but a crucial step towards establishing Jerusalem as the central place of worship for all of Israel. As the king, David recognized his responsibility to create an environment where the people of Israel could connect with God on a deeper level.

As a result, he was blessed with God's anointing and saw the Ark established in Jerusalem, the religious and political capital of the nation. David's keen understanding of his role as a leader enabled him to create a foundation of divine favor, power, and authority for his dynasty. His bloodline, through the generations, led to the ultimate fulfillment of God's promise in the form of Jesus Christ, the Messiah.

Furthermore, David's life exemplified the protocols of power, demonstrating that true leadership involves humility, obedience, and a reverence for God's authority. Despite being anointed as the future king while Saul still reigned, David refused to seize the throne by force or harm Saul in any way. Instead, he waited patiently for God's timing and trusted in His providence. David's humility and respect for God's chosen leader ultimately led to his appointment as king and secured his place in history as a man after God's own heart.

While David saw the Ark as the centerpiece of his kingdom and made it his highest priority, Saul never considered or sought after it. For Saul, God's anointing, presence, power, and throne were not priorities. We see this contrast in 1 Chronicles 13:3 (NKJV), which states, "And let us bring the Ark of our God back to us, for we have not inquired at it since the days of Saul." This verse makes it clear that Saul's reign lacked the anointing and the presence of God, while David's dynasty had the honor of having the Messiah sit on its throne. Saul's rulership lasted only twenty years, as stated in 1 Samuel 13:1. In those two decades, only two years were blessed with the anointing. This shows us that Saul's pursuit of power and his neglect of God's presence led to a shortened and less impactful rule.

In contrast, David's quest to set up the Ark as the most important priority of his kingdom speaks to his reverence for God and his desire to have His presence with him at all times. David made it a point to bring the Ark from its secluded hiding place in Kirjath Jearim to the center of his kingdom. By doing so, he not only demonstrated his commitment to God but also allowed his nation to experience the blessings and favor that come with His presence.

The difference between David and Saul goes beyond their leadership styles and priorities. It speaks to their character and their understanding of true power. While Saul relied on his own strength and cunning, David understood that true power came from surrendering to God and recognizing His authority.

David's holy bloodline would last forever, with the Messiah sitting on His throne. On the other hand, Saul's reign was marked by a lack of God's presence and anointing. The consequences of their choices and priorities were clear, with David's dynasty being blessed and remembered, while Saul's rule was forgotten and cut short.

Required Posture of the Heart

Walking in the anointing requires a posture of continual hunger and thirst for more of God. We must never become complacent or satisfied with our current level of spiritual growth. Instead, we should continually seek to deepen our relationship with God, hungering for His presence and desiring to be used by Him in greater ways. This hunger drives us to pursue spiritual disciplines such as fasting, worship, and fellowship, thereby creating an environment in which the anointing can flourish. You must embrace a life of prayer and intimacy with God, endure the refining process, and maintain a posture of continual hunger. Only those who are willing to pay this price will taste the fullness of God's anointing in their lives.

Walking in the anointing is a journey of discovering and operating in the supernatural empowerment of the Holy Spirit. It is an invitation to step into the fullness of God's purpose and to live a life that bears the mark of His divine presence. Walking in the anointing begins with a recognition of our need for the Holy Spirit's power and guidance. It is acknowledging that we cannot fulfill our calling in our own strength or wisdom. Just as a lamp needs oil to emit light, we need the anointing of the

Holy Spirit to radiate God's love, truth, and power in the world. By surrendering our lives to Him and seeking His presence, we position ourselves to receive the anointing that empowers us for the tasks and assignments God has entrusted to us.

As mentioned above, walking in the anointing requires a deepening relationship with the Holy Spirit. It involves cultivating intimacy, trust, and sensitivity to His leading. Just as a close friend knows our thoughts, desires, and preferences, the Holy Spirit desires to reveal Himself to us in a personal and intimate way. By spending time in His presence, listening to His voice, and obeying His promptings, we develop a spiritual sensitivity that enables us to discern and respond to His leading. It is in this place of communion with the Holy Spirit that we experience a deepening anointing for service.

Step Out in Faith

It is important to mention that walking in the anointing requires faith and boldness. It involves stepping out of our comfort zones, trusting in God's provision, and stepping into the opportunities He presents. The anointing of the Holy Spirit empowers us to overcome fear, insecurity, and doubt, enabling us to fulfill our calling with confidence and courage. As we step out in faith, we witness the Holy Spirit's supernatural provision, guidance, and empowerment that surpasses our own abilities.

Dear friend, pursue the call to walk in the anointing, recognizing the need for the empowerment of the Holy Spirit. May we cultivate intimacy, trust, and sensitivity to His leading. May we exercise the spiritual gifts bestowed upon us, bringing glory to God and edification to the body of Christ. May we walk in obedience and surrender, aligning our lives with God's purposes. And as we step out in faith, may we experience the supernatural provision, guidance, and empowerment of the Holy Spirit, impacting lives and fulfilling the purpose to which we have been called.

Tapping into the Power and Authority of the Holy Spirit

As believers, we have been given access to a supernatural source of power and authority through the Holy Spirit. Tapping into the power and authority of the Holy Spirit involves understanding and embracing the divine enablement that empowers us to overcome, impact, and walk in the victory that Christ has secured for us.

Tapping into the power and authority of the Holy Spirit begins with a recognition of our total dependency on Him. Knowing that without Him, we can do nothing (John 15:5). It is acknowledging that we cannot accomplish God's purposes in our own strength or wisdom. Just as a lamp needs to be connected to a power source to emit light, we need to be connected to the Holy Spirit to radiate the power and authority of God. A continual reliance on God is not a one-time experience but a daily dependency on His presence and empowerment. By consistently seeking His guidance, relying on His strength, and surrendering to His leading, we are positioned to walk in the fullness of His power and authority in every aspect of our lives.

By surrendering our lives to Him and seeking His presence, we position ourselves to receive the divine enablement that empowers us to overcome every obstacle and accomplish great things for

His glory. Understanding the power of the Holy Spirit involves recognizing that He is not a force to be controlled at will but a Person to be yielded to. The Holy Spirit is the very presence of God living within us, empowering us with supernatural abilities and resources. Just as a trusted friend stands by our side, offering their strength and support, the Holy Spirit stands with us, empowering us to fulfill our God-given calling. By developing a personal relationship with the Holy Spirit, we tap into His power, allowing Him to work in and through us to accomplish God's purposes.

Walking in Obedience and Righteousness

An essential aspect of tapping into the anointing of the Holy Spirit is walking in obedience and righteousness. It is living a life that honors God and aligns with His purposes. The power and authority of the Holy Spirit are not meant for self-centered or manipulative purposes but for the advancement of God's kingdom and the edification of others. By yielding to the Holy Spirit's guidance and living in accordance with His leading, we position ourselves to effectively wield the power and authority entrusted to us. Moreover, walking the anointing involves exercising spiritual disciplines such as prayer and fasting. These practices create space for the Holy Spirit to work in and through us, aligning our hearts and minds with God's will. By engaging in dedicated times of prayer and fasting, we open ourselves to a deeper connection with the Holy Spirit, allowing His power to flow freely and unhindered in our lives.

Beyond the Anointing

It is very important to understand that anointing alone is not enough. Without God's glory, it is incomplete and ineffective. His glory and power go hand in hand, and one without the other is an imbalance that can prove detrimental. It is the presence of God's glory that gives birth to His power within us. Just as a seed needs the right conditions to grow, so does the anointing, which requires the presence of God's glory to flourish.

The glory of God is not bestowed upon us arbitrarily. It is a gift that is conditional upon our faithfulness. When we remain loyal to God and His principles, we create an environment for His glory to dwell within us. The glory of God is not a stagnant force but a living, breathing entity that can either flourish or diminish based on our actions and choices. Therefore, it is crucial to continually seek His presence and nurture our relationship with Him.

The power that emanates from the anointing is a direct result of the glory of God. It is a gift that we receive as a consequence of His presence within us. However, it is imperative to remember that maintaining this power does not guarantee the preservation of God's glory. Throughout history, there have been instances where individuals have lost the glory while retaining power. The tragic stories of Samson and Saul serve as reminders of the importance of humility, obedience, and reverence towards God.

In the case of Samson, his disobedience and lack of regard for God's commandments ultimately led to his downfall. Despite being anointed with immense strength, his disregard for God's glory resulted in the loss of his anointing and the tragic consequences that followed. Similarly, Saul, the first king of Israel, disregarded God's instructions, leading to the removal of His glory. Although the power remained with Saul for a time, it eventually became a curse rather than a blessing.

Therefore, it is essential to understand that anointing and God's glory are interdependent. They work harmoniously, with the glory birthing the power and the power being the result of the glory. To possess the anointing without the presence of God's glory is to invite destruction into our lives. It is through the humbling of our hearts and the cultivation of a deep relationship with God that we can fully experience the anointing and its transformative power.

CHAPTER 19

BEING A GOOD STEWARD OF GOD'S PRESENCE: NURTURING THE FIRE ON THE ALTAR

The fire on the altar could represent the ongoing relationship between a believer and the father, and it signifies a connection that requires consistent attention and nurturing. Just as the fire must not go out, believers are called to actively engage with and sustain what God is doing in their lives. We are called to be good stewards of the move of God in our lives, family, church, and nations. This concept of stewardship can be seen throughout the Bible, as God instructs His people to take care of His creation and faithfully manage the resources and gifts He has entrusted to them. In the book of Leviticus, we are given a clear picture of what it means to be a good steward, as the priests were tasked with keeping the fire on the altar burning continuously.

Leviticus chapter 6, verse 13 (NIV), states, "The fire must be kept burning on the altar continuously; it must not go out." This commandment highlights the importance of diligence and faithfulness in our love and service to God. The fire on the altar was not meant to flicker or go out. Instead, it was meant to burn brightly and steadily, showing that God's power and presence were always there. As priests, it was their responsibility to tend to the fire, ensuring it never went out.

Similarly, as believers, we are called to keep the fire of our faith, prayer, and our love for the Father burning continually. We must not allow our passion for God and His work to dwindle or diminish over time. This requires intentionality and a conscious effort to regularly add "firewood" to our spiritual lives. Only dead wood can burn in the fire. Only a dead believer can keep the fire on the altar. Dead to self, Paul said, "That I may know Him and the power of His resurrection, and the fellowship of His sufferings, being conformed to His death" (Philippians 3:10, NKJV). Just as the priests were to add wood to the fire each morning, we must keep our love for God going by praying, learning God's Word, and getting together with other Christians.

Ways to Be Good Stewards

Ways to be a good steward of what God is doing is by cultivating gratitude and engaging in reflective worship. Acknowledging God's work and faithfulness through thanksgiving allows us to approach Him with a humble heart. Regular reflection and worship create an atmosphere of reverence, igniting the fire on the altar of our hearts and reminding us of God's continuous presence and blessings.

Gratitude

Gratitude, at its core, is the heartfelt acknowledgment of the blessings bestowed upon us by our Heavenly Father. It is the ability to recognize and express appreciation for the move of God, the ability to acknowledge both the big and small miracles that surround us. When we are grateful, we stop thinking about what we don't have and start thinking about what we do. We begin to view every single breath we take, every ray of sunshine, and every kind gesture as divine gifts worth cherishing. It's important to remember that being grateful doesn't mean forgetting or putting down the problems we face in life. Instead, it is about finding the silver linings and being mindful of the positive aspects that coexist with the negative. Gratitude allows us to shift our focus from what we lack to what we have, and in doing so, it enables us to experience life with a greater sense of joy and contentment. When I think about where God brought me from, where I am, and where He is taking me, I can not but whisper how grateful I am.

Nurturing through Prayer

Prayer is not merely a one-way transaction where believers seek blessings and favors from God. It is a mutual exchange of love, trust, and gratitude. It is an acknowledgment of the divine presence in every moment and a willingness to align one's life with the will of the Father. To engage in true prayer, one must cultivate a receptive and open heart. It requires humility, surrender, and a willingness to let go of ego-driven desires and attachments. True prayer is not about seeking personal gain; it is about seeking the face of God and having a desire to know His heart. Falling on our kneels daily, keeping the fire burning on the altar. The Bible says in Isaiah 62:6–7 (NKJV), "I have set watchmen on your walls, O Jerusalem; They shall never hold their peace day or night. You who make mention of the Lord, do not keep silent, And give Him no rest till He establishes And till He makes Jerusalem a praise in the earth." Sustaining the fire on the altar, we must align ourselves daily with God with our prayers.

Nurturing through Worship

True worship can be defined as the act of honoring, praising, and revering God. While true worship is commonly associated with religious practices, it goes beyond mere music and songs; it encompasses a heartfelt connection and devotion to the Heavenly Father. In today's fast-paced and materialistic world, the concept of true worship has often been overshadowed by external influences and superficial displays of singing talents. Many individuals confuse the act of worship with attending religious services and reciting prayers mechanically. However, true worship goes far beyond these external manifestations and delves into the inner realm of the soul.

True worship is an intimate encounter with God, a genuine communion between the worshipper and the worshipped. It is a deeply personal and spiritual experience that transcends religious boundaries, cultural backgrounds, and societal norms. True worship goes beyond the mere act of praising, singing songs, or performing music. It encompasses a deep and profound connection with God, a genuine expression of reverence, gratitude, and devotion towards the Father. In its essence, true worship is a heartfelt response to the divine presence.

Authentic worship is marked by sincerity and genuineness. It is a reflection of an individual's genuine love and devotion to God. It is not merely a performance or an obligation but a heartfelt expression of gratitude and reverence. True worshipers understand the significance of their actions and engage in them with utmost sincerity, knowing that their worship is an offering to God. To be a good steward of God's work, we must prioritize consistent worship and engage in spiritual disciplines.

Nurturing through Offering

Moreover, we are called to be good stewards of the offerings we bring before God. In the same verse, it is mentioned that the priests were to arrange the burnt offering on the fire and burn the fat of the fellowship offerings. These offerings represented the people's worship, prayer, and gratitude towards God. As stewards, the priests were responsible for handling and presenting these offerings in a manner that pleased God.

In our lives, the offerings we bring before God may be different, but the principle remains the same. We are to offer them to God with a heart of gratitude. However, it is not enough to simply give; we must also offer our offerings in a way that honors and pleases God. This means using our resources wisely, being generous towards others, and seeking God's guidance in how we use what He has given us.

Being a good steward of what God is doing also involves recognizing that everything we have comes from Him. The resources and opportunities we possess are not our own but rather blessings that have been entrusted to us. As stewards, we are called to manage these blessings responsibly and faithfully. This includes being wise with our finances and using our talents to make a positive impact for the glory of God. Just as the fire on the altar was to be kept burning continuously, we must keep the fire of what God is doing in our lives burning. In our places of worship, we must keep doing that which allows His presence to keep flowing. We must strive daily to keep the fire burning on the altar of our hearts and lives.

CHAPTER 20
REPRESENTING THE GOD WE KNOW

In the story of the prodigal son that I mentioned earlier in this book, the father of the prodigal son gave him a ring that symbolizes authority. The gift of a ring denotes trust, responsibility, and the granting of authority. The ring says he can act or do business on behalf of the family. The father is not only welcoming him back into the family but also acknowledging his ability to participate actively in the affairs of the household. It signifies the father's trust in his son's potential and reaffirms his position within the family structure. But we should not forget that in order for the son to use the ring, he must remain an active member of the family. We cannot represent a God that we don't know. We have many people misrepresenting God today because they have never had a relationship with the Father. Love must be the basis for any service that we give to the people of God. Many have the gift and charisma but lack character. Many can bind the devil, but they themselves have some of the enemy's properties at their disposal.

As sons and daughters of the kingdom, we have the privilege and responsibility of representing the God we know to the world around us. Our lives, actions, and attitudes can serve as a reflection of who God is and what He stands for. Representing the God we know involves living in a manner that aligns with

His character and displaying His love, grace, and truth in our interactions with others. To represent the God we know, we must first have a deep and intimate knowledge of God. This knowledge is obtained through studying His Word, spending time in prayer and worship, and cultivating a personal relationship with Him. As we grow in our understanding of who God is, His nature and attributes become ingrained in our hearts, shaping our thoughts, words, and actions.

Representing the God we know requires living a life of integrity and authenticity. It is about aligning our beliefs with our behavior and consistently demonstrating the principles and values that God has revealed to us. Just as a mirror reflects the image before it, our lives should reflect the character of God, displaying His love, righteousness, and holiness. Representing the God we know involves extending grace and compassion to others. God is a God of love and mercy, and as His representatives, we are called to mirror His compassion and forgiveness. By treating others with kindness, empathy, and respect, we demonstrate the transformative power of God's love in our own lives.

Representing the God we know also entails sharing the truth of His Word. Just as a lamp illuminates the darkness, our words and actions should shed light on God's truth. We are called to boldly and lovingly share the message of salvation, redemption, and hope found in Christ. By speaking truth in love, we invite others to experience the life-transforming power of a relationship with God. Also, representing the God we know requires living a life of humility and service. Jesus, the ultimate representation of God, modeled servant leadership, washing His disciples' feet and laying down His life for others. By humbly serving those around us, we reflect the heart of God and point others to His selfless love.

In a nutshell, representing the God we know involves seeking reconciliation and promoting unity. God is a God of reconciliation, and He calls us to be peacemakers in a divided world. By seeking to bridge divides, fostering understanding, and pursuing reconciliation, we demonstrate the transformative power of God's love in healing relationships and bringing about unity. In all our endeavors to represent the God we know, it is important to remember that we are imperfect vessels. We will make mistakes and fall short at times. Yet, God's grace is abundant, and He is ever willing to use us despite our weaknesses. As we surrender to His work within us, relying on His strength and guidance, we can grow in our ability to accurately represent Him to the world.

May we be intentional in representing the God we know, living lives that reflect His character, extending grace and compassion, sharing His truth, serving others, seeking reconciliation, and promoting unity. By doing so, we become vessels through which others can encounter the transformative power of God's love, and His glory can shine through us for all to see.

Sharing the Love and Truth of God with the World

As human beings, we have been entrusted with a powerful message, a message of God's love, grace, and truth. We are called to share this message with the world, to be ambassadors of God's kingdom and bearers of His light. Sharing the love and truth of God is not merely a duty but a privilege and a calling that requires a heart full of compassion and a desire to make a positive impact on the lives of others. When we share the love and truth of God, we become conduits of His grace, extending His love to a hurting and broken world. Just as a smile can brighten someone's day, a kind word or act of love can touch hearts and bring hope to those in need. By demonstrating acts of kindness, compassion, and generosity, we reflect God's love and draw others to Him.

Sharing the love and truth of God also involves living a life of authenticity and transparency. It is about being open and honest about our own struggles, failures, and need for God's grace. As we share our own stories of redemption and transformation, we create a safe space for others to do the same. Through our vulnerability, we show that God's love is not reserved for the perfect but for all who are willing to receive it. In sharing the love and truth of God, we must be attentive to the needs and concerns of those around us. We listen with compassion and empathy, seeking to understand their unique experiences and challenges. By meeting people where they are, we can offer the love and truth of God in ways that resonate with their hearts and minds.

Moreover, sharing the love and truth of God requires us to speak truth with love. We communicate God's Word in a way that is compassionate, respectful, and relevant to the lives of others. By addressing their deepest needs and questions, we invite them into a conversation that can lead to a deeper understanding of God's love and truth. Sharing the love and truth of God is not limited to words alone; it also involves living a life of integrity and consistency. Our actions should align with our beliefs, reflecting the transformative work of God in our lives. By living out our faith in tangible ways, we provide a living testimony of God's love and truth.

Finally, sharing the love and truth of God requires reliance on the Holy Spirit. We recognize that it is not our own eloquence or persuasiveness that brings about transformation but the work of the Holy Spirit in the hearts of people. We rely on His guidance, wisdom, and power to open hearts, reveal truth, and draw others to a personal relationship with God. As we embrace the privilege and responsibility of sharing the love and truth of God, we become vessels through which His love and truth flow. We are called to be salt and light in the world, impacting lives and pointing others to the source of true hope and transformation. May we humbly and faithfully share the love and truth of God with the world, knowing that it is through His love and truth that lives are changed, hearts are healed, and souls are saved.

Impacting Others through Intimacy with the Heavenly Father

As human beings, we have a natural longing for deep and meaningful connections. One of the most profound ways we can impact others is through our intimacy with the Heavenly Father. When we cultivate a close relationship with God, His love, wisdom, and grace overflow from our lives, touching the lives of those around us. Our intimacy with the Heavenly Father begins by prioritizing time in His presence. Just as we invest time in nurturing relationships with our loved ones, we must invest time in communing with God. Through prayer, worship, and studying His Word, we create space for intimacy to flourish. As we spend time in His presence, our hearts are transformed, and we become vessels through which His love can flow.

Intimacy with the Heavenly Father impacts others through the power of example. When we display a genuine love for God, it becomes contagious, inspiring others to seek Him as well. Our lives become a living testimony of God's goodness, faithfulness, and grace. As we navigate life's challenges and triumphs, we demonstrate the peace and joy that comes from a close relationship with the Father, drawing others into the embrace of His love. Through our intimacy with the Heavenly Father, we also become conduits of His wisdom and guidance. As we seek His counsel and align our hearts with His will, we are empowered to offer wise and discerning insights to those around us. Our words become a source of encouragement, comfort, and direction, pointing others toward the Heavenly Father, who holds all wisdom and understanding.

Intimacy with the Heavenly Father leads us to carry His heart for the broken and marginalized. As we intimately know His compassion and love, we are compelled to extend the same to others. Our intimacy with God fuels our passion for justice, mercy, and reconciliation. We become advocates for the oppressed, the hurting, and the marginalized, bringing hope and healing to their lives. Furthermore, intimacy with the Heavenly Father equips us to love unconditionally.

God's love transcends human limitations and embraces all people, regardless of their background, struggles, or failures. As we intimately experience His love, we are transformed to love others in the same way. Our relationships become characterized by acceptance, forgiveness, and grace, impacting others with the transformative power of God's love. Intimacy with the Heavenly Father also strengthens our faith and boldness. When we intimately know His faithfulness and presence, we are emboldened to step out in obedience and take risks for His kingdom. Our lives become marked by a fearless pursuit of God's purposes, inspiring others to step into their own God-given destinies.

In impacting others through our intimacy with the Heavenly Father, we must always remember that it is God who ultimately works in and through us. We are vessels, imperfect yet chosen to carry His love and truth. As we surrender to His leading and allow His love to flow through us, we become instruments of His grace, impacting lives and bringing glory to His name.

Dear friend, cultivate intimacy with the Heavenly Father and allow His love and presence to permeate your life. May our intimacy with Him be a catalyst for transformation in the lives of others. May we impact others through the example of our lives, the wisdom we share, the compassion we extend, and the unconditional love we offer. May our intimacy with the Heavenly Father inspire others to seek Him, knowing that in Him, they too can find the deep connection and fulfillment their hearts long for.

CONCLUSION
EMBRACING A LIFE OF INTIMACY WITH GOD

As I reflect on the journey we have taken in exploring intimacy with God, I am reminded of the profound impact it can have on our lives. Embracing a life of intimacy with God is not a mere religious practice; it is a transformative journey that touches every aspect of our being. Through intimacy with God, we come to know Him as our Heavenly Father—a loving and compassionate presence who desires to walk closely with us. He extends an invitation to us into a relationship that is characterized by deep connection, trust, and openness. In this relationship, we discover a source of unconditional love, wisdom, and guidance that surpasses all human understanding.

Intimacy with God changes the way we see ourselves. It reveals our true identity as beloved children of God, created with purpose and destined for greatness. As we draw near to Him, we experience healing, restoration, and transformation. Our fears and insecurities are replaced with confidence and hope. We realize that we are not defined by our past or our circumstances but by the incredible love and grace of our Heavenly Father. Embracing a life of intimacy with God also impacts our relationships with others. As we experience God's love, we are empowered to love others selflessly and sacrificially. Our relationships become characterized by compassion, forgiveness, and reconciliation. We become agents of healing and restoration, extending God's grace and truth to those around us.

Intimacy with God gives us a fresh perspective on life. It enables us to see beyond the temporal and embrace the eternal. We gain wisdom and discernment to navigate life's challenges and make choices that align with God's purposes. We find peace and contentment knowing that our lives are in the hands of a loving and sovereign God. However, intimacy with God is not a destination but a lifelong journey. It requires intentionality, discipline, and a genuine desire to draw near to Him. It calls us to set aside time for prayer, worship, and the study of His Word. It invites us to surrender our will and align our desires with His. It challenges us to live a life of obedience and faith, trusting in His guidance and provision.

As I conclude, I encourage you to embrace a life of intimacy with God. Allow the Holy Spirit to draw you to the place of communion. Seek Him with all your heart, knowing that He eagerly awaits your presence. Embrace the invitation to draw near to Him and experience His love, His grace, and His transformational power. Allow His truth to shape your thoughts, His wisdom to guide your decisions, and His presence to fill every aspect of your life. Remember, the journey of intimacy with God is not always easy. There will be moments of struggle, doubt, and uncertainty. But in those moments, hold on to the truth that God is faithful. He is with you every step of the way, walking alongside you, strengthening you, and empowering you to live a life that reflects His love and truth.

May your journey of intimacy with God be marked by a deepening love, a growing faith, and an unwavering trust in His goodness. May you experience the joy, peace, and fulfillment that come from knowing Him intimately. May your life be a living testimony of the transformative power of a life surrendered to the embrace of the Heavenly Father.

THE FINAL WORD

It is very important that I end this book on this note that God wants to be found. Deep down inside, every one of us has a longing to experience the closeness of a power that is more significant than ourselves. We look for a meaning and a purpose in life by asking ourselves some of the most fundamental questions. The Holy Scriptures teach us that even though it is in God's nature to conceal Himself, He nevertheless gives us the opportunity to search for Him, even though this may appear to be a contradiction. Seeking is the only way that will allow us to have a genuine encounter with the presence of God.

The book of Isaiah reminds us of this hidden nature of God, declaring, "Verily thou art a God that hidest thyself, O God of Israel, the Saviour" (Isaiah 45:15, NKJV). This verse serves as a reminder that the path to finding God is a journey that requires effort and perseverance. It is not a simple task but rather one that requires commitment and dedication. "You will seek me and find me when you seek me with all your heart" (Jeremiah 29:13, NIV). He desires for us to make the effort to find Him. This is not a test of His love for us but a testament to His desire for an intimate relationship with His creation. The privilege rests in our hands to actively seek Him, to engage in the pursuit of His presence.

The Song of Solomon provides a vivid illustration of this pursuit. The writer, in search of the one her soul loves, seeks him passionately but initially comes up empty-handed. However, her persistence pays off, and she eventually finds the object of her affection. This story holds a powerful message for us—that the longer and more earnestly we search for God, the more of ourselves we lose in the process. The pursuit of God must ultimately lead to the death of self, stripping away our own desires and ego in favor of His will.

Solomon's delay in revealing himself until he was certain of the seeker's seriousness teaches us an important lesson. God wants to see how dedicated and determined we are in our search for Him. He does not want half-hearted devotion; instead, He desires our complete surrender. It is only when we lay everything aside and wholeheartedly pursue Him that we will find what we are truly seeking.

There is a price to pay in acquiring the power of God—prayer, dedication, surrender, and obedience. These are not light commitments but rather the necessary sacrifices for a deeper connection with our Creator. Through prayer, we open up a line of communication with God, allowing Him to speak to us and guide our steps. Dedication requires a persistent and unwavering pursuit of Him, even when it becomes challenging or seemingly fruitless. Surrender entails letting go of our own desires and submitting completely to His will. And finally, obedience is essential in following His commands and living out His Word.

God wants to be found, but He also wants us to desire Him enough to put in the effort to seek Him. In this search, we discover the true essence of our being and experience the power and presence of God in our lives. So let us press on, with determination and persistence, knowing that the reward for our search is a closer and more intimate relationship with the Creator of the universe.

God's withdrawal is not an act of cruelty or indifference. Rather, it is a divine invitation for us to follow. It is through this process of seeking and struggling that we grow in our faith and draw closer to God. The journey may be long and challenging, but the reward of finding Him is immeasurable. We must be willing to let go of ourselves, to die to our own desires, and to seek Him with all our hearts, for it is in this search that we truly find the essence of God's love and presence in our lives. So, let us embark on this profound journey, knowing that God is waiting for us to find Him. God bless you!

Music Album: New Day

Music Album: Baruch Haba

Intimacy With God

Book: When the Going Gets Tough

ABOUT THE AUTHOR

Femi Agboola is a minister, worship leader, author, revivalist, and a man of God's presence. He has a deep passion for Jesus and a genuine desire to see people transformed by His power and love. As an Information Technology professional, he leverages his experience to reach people all over the world. Femi has been in the ministry from his teenage years, serving in various capacities in and out of the church setting. He is passionate about teaching God's people how to experience and steward God's presence.

Femi believes that life with God is meant to be an adventure. He is passionate about seeing individuals and the body of Christ genuinely connected with God in an intimate relationship with Him.

Together, Femi and his wife, Yemi, are founders of the One-Way TV network. They have a strong desire to see the value of the kingdom of heaven manifested here on earth. They serve the body of Christ through ministering the Word and intense worship that brings the presence of God. Their monthly prayer program (Living Spring Prayer Network) draws many believers from various backgrounds. Through this endeavor, Femi and Yemi create a space where individuals can come together to seek God's face, intercede for their communities, and experience the supernatural power of prayer.

Femi's ministry and relationship with God are indispensable to his life's work, and he incorporates them into his role as a husband and father. Femi and Yemi are blessed with four wonderfully blessed children: Ayo, Tope, Femi, and Dara. They recognize the immense responsibility of raising their children in an environment that instills strong Christian values and teaches them to live out their faith in a practical and meaningful way.